LEADING THE WAR

Salvation Army Officership
as Vocational Extremism

JAMES KNAGGS AND STEPHEN COURT

Leading the War
Salvation Army Officership as Vocational Extremism
James Knaggs and Stephen Court
2015 Frontier Press

Knaggs, James
Court, Stephen
Leading the War

September 2015

ISBN 978-0-9908776-4-6
Printed in the United States on recycled paper

frontier press

THE SALVATION ARMY USA WESTERN TERRITORY

Dedication

This book is dedicated to the faithful soldiers of The Salvation Army. May those soldiers who step into covenantal officership model vocational extremism in relationship with you.

Acknowledgements

What makes this book special is the personal and spiritual contributions of the 26 Salvation Army officers who have taken the time to invest in the current cadre of officers worldwide and the future cadets and officers of The Salvation Army by responding to our five questions.

Thanks also to Majors Marney and Len Turner and to the editorial staff at Frontier Press.

TABLE OF CONTENTS

PART ONE

REALLY?

Really? Officership as vocational extremism? Are you kidding? No, we're not.

We're pretty tired of hearing people slam officership. Just recently Steve received an email about the soft, cushy, secure jobs that officers enjoy.

Sure, some people sign on because of what they see as the "perks." But they quickly find out that the lifestyle is far more demanding than they bargained for. And it bothers us that some officers don't demonstrate that officership is the most attractive, captivating way to throw away your life. It bothers us more when soldiers don't even consider officership. The devil has really put one over on us to have devised such disdain toward and disregard for the vocation.

Yet we know there are soldiers (officers included) who are sold out and committed to winning the world for Jesus. If you're in this group, what you read here will inspire you, no doubt. If you're not, if you know Jesus but have just not completely surrendered your life to him, read on. On the other hand, if you're satisfied with following Jesus "at a distance" (Matthew 26:58), you can lend your copy to someone else and grab the remote. This book is definitely not for you.

NO OPTION
You probably agree that officership is a calling. But you may dismiss

out of hand the idea of officership as vocational extremism. If so, you need to pay attention to what we and the other officers in this book have to say. "Being at war is always tough!" says Major Kjell Karlsten of Sweden. "We're in a battle," says Lt. Colonel Miriam Gluyas, now serving in Papua New Guinea. "The devil hates it when God's at work. I expect the battle."

But it's not like you have an option. That's right, you have no option. If you're still reading, you're not some slacker pew sitter who responded to an earnest appeal by some preacher to accept Jesus with a casual, "Yeah, I'll take some" and never graduated beyond an occasional "Daily Bread" devotional book reading.

You love Jesus. You're an active soldier or officer. And you know what? You have no option.

> Are all to become officers? Yes, all who are adapted for it. We go on the lines of adaptation. If you are cut out for being an Officer, an Officer you must be, and an Officer you will be, or it will be so much the worse for you both here and hereafter.
> —William Booth, *The General's Letters*, 1885

You see, we only want what's best for you! And officership as vocational extremism is definitely the best kind of life any soldier can imagine. "I am completely resolved that there is nothing else I want to do with my life than to be an officer and to serve God through this vocation," says retired Commissioner Raymond Finger of Australia. "It was to this end that I was born and to this purpose that I shall die."

Officers form a cadre of mighty warriors. Major Danielle Strickland of Canada says that one amazing thing about officership is "the fellowship of the fight." "I do not want to miss out on making history as we advance the Kingdom of God," says Major Shar Davis of New Zealand. But maybe you are an officer and you're wondering in what century we, the authors, are fighting! Officership is vocational extremism? Not sold? Read the rest of the book.

SATURATED INTENSITY

Think about it for a minute. You get to invest all your energies, all your passion, all your gifts and skills and abilities toward the fulfillment of the mission to win the world for Jesus. So your days will be filled with prayer, Bible saturation, evangelism, and discipleship. There's no down time for officers. "I love the fact that I get to be in relationship with Jesus, that I get to spend time with Him every day, and that I get to partner up with Him in seeing His Kingdom come and His will be done," says Colonel Gluyas. "There's nothing better than that." Colonel Barbara Hunter of the U.S. says the best thing about officership for her is "the fact that I am able to serve 24/7. ... God can call on me any time of the day—that's great."

TAKE NOTE: In this section and throughout this book, we are projecting the ideal of Salvation Army officership. There would be little point in writing a book celebrating the lowest common denominator of mediocre officership.

We know a few officers who used to be totally committed but after years of apparent drudgery and frustration have become distracted by the world's pleasures and comforts and have lost their focus, their zeal for souls, and their passion for Jesus. As Commissioner Wesley Harris of the UK puts it, "Some may abandon officership not so much because of overstrain, but because of "under-motive." Other officers have settled into a routine of life and lifestyle, having turned officership into a career. (We have reprinted the officer's covenant in an appendix as a reminder.)

We know a few soldiers who are afraid to sign up because they want to protect their freedom. They've missed the boat. Biblical freedom comes only when we sell ourselves into slavery. Slavery to Jesus is freedom. It's the Gospel paradox. Until these "freedom lovers" sign up, they'll never optimize their impact, never accomplish God's Plan A for them.

Sure, there are other things you could do. You could get rich and donate a billion dollars to The Salvation Army. You could invent a drug that would cure AIDS. You could get famous running around a football field.

Now, you may be called by God to work in a secular profession. Fine. Fantastic, even. God bless you. But you should do that AS a soldier. Salvation Army soldiership is the most covenanted life we know of. The Articles of War—A Soldier's Covenant—feature spiritual footnotes that run to two full books: the *Orders and Regulations for Soldiers* and the *Handbook of Doctrine*. Soldiership is hard core. And local officers and other soldiers are models to the world. We love soldiership. And every officer is fundamentally a soldier. Officership is not better than soldiership. But it is more rarely pursued. So, know that we completely agree that God calls some to be faithful soldiers and local officers while serving as butchers and bus drivers and CPAs and CEOs.

But if you know God is calling you to be an officer, you have no option. All other pursuits will be completely unsatisfying. They will pale in comparison with leading warriors in the eternal conflict against the devil and his armies. Commissioner Garth McKenzie of New Zealand once faced such a choice, and he left worldly success behind.

> I was due to receive my 10-year service pen from the managing director of my company, with the expectation of a gold watch after 30 years of service. However, the Spirit of God compelled me to respond to the invitation on a Sunday evening of commissioning as I sensed a clear word in my mind to be an officer.

LEADING THE WAR

It's your responsibility to prepare for officership as vocational extremism. Every good soldier (officers included) prepares for officership in the hope that she/he will be considered qualified to take on vocational leadership in the "fist" of the body of Christ (aka The Salvation Army).

> Why should the War suffer? Why should the enemy triumph? Why should the battle languish for want of leaders when you are the very people—possess the very gifts—have been saved for the very purpose of carrying it on?
> —William Booth, *The General's Letters*, 1885

Exactly. And there's no life like it. You are best positioned to fulfill the mission as a mighty warrior officer. There are no worldly entrapments. There are no limitations or restrictions. There is nothing but the prospect of much hot and furious fighting, saving souls from hell for heaven forever, and ultimate victory and glory pay. Vocational extremism.

So, what we're saying, from experience, is that there is absolutely nothing we'd rather be doing—except to be doing it better. We have friends who make big money in the world. But how can a paycheck compare to leading the Army of God, building the body of Christ, guiding the family of God, heading up construction of the Temple of God?

CAN'T HACK IT?

When Steve's grandfather was nearing his promotion to Glory, the lieutenant colonel counseled his grandson, "Don't become a Salvation Army officer unless you can't do anything else." He meant that officership is so hard, so demanding, so utterly radical that it would ruin him unless God would absolutely not let him survive in any other pursuit. The "can't" was an existential warning, as in "can't be fulfilled or can't be at peace in any other line of work." Tragically, Steve heard it as utilitarian: "If you can't get a half-decent job, then become an officer."

Thankfully, God clarified things pretty quickly for Steve. But far too many Salvationists—officers and other soldiers alike—embrace this same delusion when it comes to what is essentially the most extreme leadership lifestyle imaginable. Too many Salvationists, when considering the next batch of cadets, figure, "I guess s/he couldn't hack it in the real world."

Rather than value officership, some Salvationists harbor ambitions of worldly success. It's as if the gifts that God has generously given them can only be authenticated by the accoutrements of secular achievement.

HACKING IT IN THE CORPORATE WORLD

We've heard people criticize Salvation Army officers, saying they couldn't hack it in the corporate world. That lie screams out for a response. Here is one:

"We have fantastic quality leaders in The Salvation Army, both at the officer level and local officer level." So says Phil Wall, founder of Signify Ltd, a leadership consultancy (and legendary Salvo) in the October 2007 *Pipeline*. But that isn't enough. Here's a bit more.

- First up, loyalty. Corporate leaders are committed, often, not to the company, but to the dollar. Officers are committed not to the dollar but to the Lord through the Army.
- Second, commitment. Corporate leaders work crazy hours for their wealthy lifestyles and perks beyond mention. Officers are literally on call all the time for modest to humble lifestyles beyond reproach. And we know 80 hour/weekers in both streams.
- Third, professionalism. Corporate leaders epitomize professionalism. Officers act in a professional manner, and many officers lead organizations larger than most companies.
- Fourth, social skills. Corporate leaders are usually quite adept within their social strata. Officers often straddle the divide between wealthy and homeless and operate effectively within both spheres.
- Fifth, impact. Corporate leaders raise wealth for shareholders. Officer leaders transform lives, care for people, make disciples, and reform.

(Officers: You might want to re-read that section.)

HACKING IT IN OFFICERSHIP

Maybe we should ask if corporate leaders could hack it in officership. Such a questionnaire might read as follows:

- First, sacrifice. Are you prepared to give up the fancy home, fancy car, sensational perks, wonderful vacations, and other creature comforts associated with your job?
- Second, skill base. Can you counsel pastorally in the morning, evangelize door-to-door in the afternoon, preach in the evening, and write a budget at night? (And maybe serve meals on the street at midnight or play basketball with the teens, like one CO we know)
- Third, love. Will you be motivated by love for the down and out, the more fragile in our communities?
- Fourth, availability. Are you prepared to pick up and move at the command of your boss tomorrow? Anywhere? Without question?
- Fifth, humility. Are you able to submit your ambition to the will of the organization?

If any corporate leaders can answer "yes" to these five questions, AND if they submit their lives to Jesus and get discipled and trained up as soldiers, then they qualify for the vocational extremism that is officership. At that point, it is a matter of deciding which "business" deserves their time and attention. Here is how William Booth explained it:

> My business is to get the world saved; If this involves the standing still of the looms and the shutting up of the factories and the staying of the sailing of the ships, let them all stand still. When we have got everybody converted, they can go on again.
> —William Booth, *The War Cry*, December 20, 1884

The issue is spiritual and it deals with priorities. Listen to President Theodore Roosevelt:

It is not the critic who counts; not the man who points out how the strong man stumbles, or where the doer of deeds could have done them better. The credit belongs to the man who is actually in the arena, whose face is marred by dust and sweat and blood; who strives valiantly; who errs, who comes short again and again, because there is no effort without error and shortcoming; but who does actually strive to do the deeds; who knows great enthusiasms, the great devotions; who spends himself in a worthy cause; who at the best knows in the end the triumph of high achievement, and who at the worst, if he fails, at least fails while daring greatly, so that his place shall never be with those cold and timid souls who neither know victory nor defeat.

—From the speech, "Citizenship in a Republic," delivered April 23, 1910, at the Sorbonne

If you are slightly vexed by the foregoing, maybe you can relate to Bronwyn's situation.

BRONWYN'S DILEMMA

Bronwyn is very successful. Having graduated at the top of her class, with awards and scholarships in tow, she continued her education at one of the top law schools in the country. As a member of a prestigious downtown law firm, Bronwyn consistently receives high evaluations and extra responsibility.

She is happily married to a wonderful husband. They enjoy the fruits of two substantial incomes. They are both witty and attractive and Christian. Yet Bronwyn is disillusioned.

What's wrong? Isn't this the ideal situation? Bronwyn is wealthy, healthy, and born again to boot! No doubt the local congregation appreciates the massive 10 percent contribution she drops in the plate each Sunday. How could someone so successful still be disillusioned?

We're warning you, the answer may hurt. It may hit a bit too close to home. Bronwyn complains that all she sees is work, groceries, and laundry. A brilliant person, and all she's got to show for her life is work, groceries, and laundry. Understandably, this frustrates her, dissatisfies her, leaves her discontented.

To be blunt, the answer for her is surrender. Full surrender. Yes, Bronwyn gave her heart to Jesus when she was young. Yes, she faithfully attends her place of worship and "pulls her weight" for the congregation. Yes, she reads her Bible and prays. Jesus has forgiven Bronwyn's sins, adopted her into His family. She's going to Heaven. But it's on her terms, not Jesus' terms.

Bronwyn is positioned to succeed impressively according to the world's values. But she has the capacity to make a huge impact on this generation for Jesus. She needs to fully surrender control of her life.

Of course, full surrender would require a different lifestyle. Her priorities must be Jesus first, then family, then work, and so on. She needs to be willing to go anywhere, do anything, anytime, for Jesus. Right now, there are limits to her commitment. Right now, there is a framework in which Bronwyn dictates how God can work. But God is not prepared to make any deals. When Bronwyn starts eating, sleeping, and breathing Jesus, He'll be free to transform her.

The key change with full surrender will be the Holy Spirit filling her. She won't need to wait long. The Holy Spirit will quickly come and invade her whole being, filling her with love, joy, and peace. He can transform her immense talents into powerful gifts that can be used effectively for His glory—but only on His terms.

The Holy Spirit also fills the void, the discontent of an endless string of weeks full of work, groceries, and laundry. No longer will disillusionment and dissatisfaction be the hallmarks of her life.

We don't know if you can relate to Bronwyn. But when you look back over the weeks and months, what do you have to show for them? Are there significant changes in your neighborhood (and up in Heaven) because of what you are doing here? If not, why not surrender, fully? Let the Holy Spirit invade you and let Him set the agenda.

Bronwyn has a friend who did that, and he ended up quitting a professional career in finance to become a missionary living on volunteer financial support. Bronwyn knows another person, a Salvationist, who gives most of her income to God, in faith, and multiplies the effects of her life beyond the city in which she lives.

There are several billion people rushing headlong into hell. Many have died between the day this was written and the day it was published. Many of them are living in your backyard.

Don't you want to make a bigger difference?

We're not saying that the bigger difference must be through officership. And we're not saying that full surrender leading to being filled by the Holy Spirit inevitably leads to officership.

But what we're saying is also not "business as usual." This is not last generation's officership that we're pitching to you here. There is no better means for someone to make a bigger impact in the world than officership as vocational extremism. Pray it out. If God is not calling you to be investing your hours and years and skills and gifts and abilities and passions in your current employment, train up and offer yourself for officership—as vocational extremism. Is God tapping you on the shoulder? Major Ivan Bezzant of New Zealand expresses the richness of that calling.

> Now consider God looking out upon creation and choosing leaders of leaders to lead this work—and He chooses you. Wow! God knows all about your weaknesses, yet He calls you to lead in this great endeavor for His Kingdom. This must be the best thing about being a Salvation Army officer. To join in this mission along with your spiritual ancestors who have carried the vision, to honor their part in the journey, and now to take hold of your moment in history and live with eyes on the past, serving the present, and reaching into the future to pass on to the next generation of officers the mantle of leadership of this great work.

FIVE QUESTIONS

We're convinced that Salvation Army officership, properly under-stood and lived out, is a wild adventure of faith (spelled R–I–S–K?) and hurt and pain and joy and gratitude. It smashes the American dream and its corollaries right in the face. It is fully alive. In fact, ideally, it is life in the extreme:

- **Extreme in emotion.** You get front row seats to the harshest of human situations in death, in fracture, in failure, in sickness, in addiction, in sin. You also get a backstage pass to celebrations of salvation and sanctification, to covenant and community.
- **Extreme in demand.** You are never off duty. The charity employees and social workers with whom officers are sometimes mistakenly compared go home at the end of the workday and assume private identity and enjoy personal freedom. Not so the officer.
- **Extreme in reimbursement.** You are promised nothing, guaranteed nothing beyond, at best, a very modest lifestyle. You build no equity. The perks are that people at airports and in alleys "recognize" you and call on you for help.

And it is vocational extremism. "Advancement," "promotion," "career," "equity," "comfort" are foreign words in the officership vocabulary. Management guru Peter Drucker calls officers "venture capitalists" because we throw a lot of our resources—energy, time, heart, money—at some high-risk "capital"—the lives of hurting and broken people—with the potential of a great payoff—they get saved and healed and back on the right track. Great call.

But we don't want you to take our word for it. So we have asked 26 officers who have fully surrendered, who have a track record of officership as vocational extremism, five questions:

1. What's the best thing about being a Salvation Army officer?

2. What keeps you in officership when things are tough?

3. What is the greatest move of God you have experienced in an appointment?

4. What's the best innovation you've helped create or extend?

5. What's the best means of influence and how have you used it?

Weigh what they say. Their answers should prove encouraging for you if you are frustrated, inspiring for you if you are in a rut, challenging for you if you are not yet committed. … Read on.

PART TWO

CALLED AS A COUPLE

GENERAL PAUL A RADER

1. What is the best thing about being a Salvation Army officer?

The life of the officer is such a rich and varied experience that it is difficult to fix upon one feature as most rewarding or significant. There is the diversity of opportunity, such a remarkable range of ministry options; the global reach of the Army and the platform for cross-cultural mission it affords; the remarkable camaraderie we share around the world with fellow officers; the freedom to innovate; the joy of proclaiming a powerful Gospel that is the power of God unto salvation and then seeing the transformation it brings to redeemed lives; the deep satisfaction of living out a calling that is of eternal consequence. But if I were to select one, it would be the privilege of working side by side with our spouses as partners in marriage and ministry.

God called Kay and me to officership as a couple. We trained as a couple. And we have been privileged to serve as a team all across the years. We have been able to augment and integrate our individual mix of gifts. My wife has a special gift for insight and wise counsel that has been invaluable to me, quite apart from her evident teaching, preaching, and leadership gifts. She has been my spiritual chaplain and partner in prayer and the walk of faith. It is part of the genius of the Army to enable us to strengthen one another in this way. Working together, by God's grace, we have been able to navigate the challenges of fulfilling our ministry responsibilities while raising a family of children who know and love the Lord.

2. What keeps you in officership when things are tough?

The call, the commission, the covenant. And beyond these, a sense of privilege at being called to this ministry. We have had our share of disappointments and disillusionments. But the privilege of association with courageous and godly officers and comrades has far outweighed the difficulties. We have often thought, *God called us in and it will take God to call us out of this spiritual vocation.* We were blessed with a succession of godly leaders during our early service in Korea. Our first training principal, Lt. Colonel Kwon Kynung-chan, under whom we served at the college until his retirement, was a remarkable officer and leader. We joined a staff at the officer training college in Seoul that included three Korean-born couples who later served as territorial leaders for the Korea Territory. We felt privileged to work beside them. That sense of privilege has never left us.

3. What is the greatest move of God you have experienced in an appointment?

We were privileged to be a part of a period of explosive growth of the Army in Korea. It came at the end of a long and discouraging period when the territory was statistically flat-lined. The time was right. I had just returned from two years of study and preparation of a strategy for growth. There was widespread concern for growth among our officers and soldiers. The leadership was committed. All that was required was a spark. We met together for a territorial growth strategy conference. But pessimism prevailed. Then, as we poured out our hearts to the Lord and shared our frustrations and our desperate desire to see the Army move forward, suddenly God broke in on the proceedings. Inspired by the Spirit, the field secretary declared, "We can, if we will!" The whole spirit of the meetings was transformed. Spirit-born optimism took hold. Bold plans were proposed. Commitments were made and, from that point forward, the Army in Korea was again on the march. It was a *kairos* moment.

4. What is the best innovation you have helped to create or extend?

Pursuing growth initiatives in Korea and in the USA Western Territory required exploring the legitimacy and practicality of planting differing models of corps life and ministry. We experimented with New Life Centers, which began with evangelistic outreach in the expectation that engagement with social needs in the community would emerge out of the life of our corps people. We encouraged the development of recovery corps in the West centering on Adult Rehabilitation Centers. In Korea we initiated a revolving fund for providing seed money to new plants. Web-based interconnectedness of all territories and commands through Lotus Notes was introduced on our watch, along with major changes in the status of married women officers. All of these innovations depended upon the creative involvement of teams of gifted people committed to growth and willing to take risks. The task of leadership was to keep the green lights on through the system and the goal clearly in view.

5. What is the best means of influence and how have you used it?

Leadership in the Army is about character. Character makes moral influence possible. Some things require the exercise of positional prerogatives. And without question positional authority has its place. But ultimately it is moral authority that engenders trust. And trust is crucial to securing an enduring commitment to realizing the vision of the leadership.

Building trust requires consistency, a measure of competence, a demonstrated awareness of the issues, capturing and casting a clear vision for the future, and compassion. I have tried in my leadership to operate within that paradigm, leaning heavily on competent and committed staff not afraid to push the envelope, and depending on the faithfulness of God.

GENERAL PAUL A. RADER, of the USA Eastern Territory, was elected to the Army's highest office as worldwide leader on July 23, 1994, and served until 1999. He earned B.A., B.D., M.Th., and D.Miss. degrees (and was awarded an LL.D. from Asbury College) and served for 22 years in the Korea Territory as well as in training and leadership appointments in the USA Eastern and Western Territories.

As international leaders, General Paul and Commissioner Kay F. Rader, driven by their fervent belief in the scriptural imperative to take the Gospel to all the world and in the success of church growth principles, set bold, imaginative targets for expansionary growth. They extended the work in the USA Western Territory into the South Pacific, which added diverse ethnic ministries. They had a clear vision of the challenge facing the Army and of the need for soldiers and officers to be clean, pure vessels for the Spirit if they were to minister effectively.

THRILLED TO BE INCLUDED

COMMISSIONER JAMES KNAGGS

1. What is the best thing about being a Salvation Army officer?

I believe the mission of The Salvation Army is so much in sync with the Gospel and the plan of God that I am thrilled to be included. Officership for me includes accepting my Army appointments as from God Himself. This sets me free to move at the moment of the farewell and the new appointment. I don't have to sweat the appointment to determine if it is right for me or not. I just go with the full intention to prove God right. He knows how to work the Army system. I trust Him implicitly.

2. What keeps you in officership when things are tough?

I know this is where God wants me. Why would I let anyone or any situation distract me from my calling in Christ Jesus?

When I was a divisional youth and candidates secretary in Greater New York, I had a patch where I was a little down. I really don't recall why. Sitting at home that night, I began to check the want ads for other employment. I had had enough. I didn't need The Salvation Army to complete my life. *The New York Times* has a large want ad section, so I had plenty of choices to look over.

Because I like to work with people, I went right to the Personnel section. Today it would likely be called Human Resources. The jobs looked promising, and I believed I had the credentials to give it a go. But as I sat there, I thought about how difficult it would be to share my faith with people. Most employers wouldn't tolerate it in such a role.

I then thought, *Well, I really love to present the Gospel. I think I'll look into the ministry opportunities.* Yes, there were quite a few of these as well. With my theological bias towards holiness and Arminianism, I looked past the Baptist and Episcopalian-type openings. I wondered if there might be Missionary Alliance or Nazarene ministries available. Even with a few of these, it occurred to me as I pondered the possibilities that I really like The Salvation Army and fit there best.

The paper dropped to my lap as my arms rested from my honest searching. I closed my eyes to thank God for this gentle and patient reminder to my soul that He had called me to The Salvation Army and if He wanted me to do something else, He would tell me so.

3. What is the greatest move of God you have experienced in an appointment?

I see the movement of God every day in officership. Would we minimize the salvation of a single soul, simply because there have been times when more than one were saved? Of course not.

Among the many great meetings where hundreds have flowed to the Mercy Seat in holy streams and where many have offered themselves for full-time service in The Salvation Army, there have, as well, been supernatural healings that God has transacted in front of our very eyes. I recall a pivotal point in one corps appointment in Wilkes-Barre, Pennsylvania.

As young officers, we had been working hard to demonstrate that

God would bless our efforts, large and small, if we offered them to Him. Our budget was strained and we had heavy financial obligations that were causing anxiety among us. At a soldiers meeting, we shared from the Gospels about the use of talents and how two stewards had doubled their holdings for the Lord while one buried his for safekeeping. Carolyn and I then placed $300 in one-dollar bills on the Holiness Table for the people to take as they needed as a gift from God. We agreed that at the end of 30 days we would take up an offering and see how God had blessed these resources dedicated to Him.

What the congregation didn't know was that the money was from our personal bank account, which we had nearly emptied to prove the provision of God. I expected to simply take back the money at the end of the faith exercise until I realized that we had to give it to the Lord for Him to bless. There was no taking it back. We went to silent prayer while the corps sergeant-major played a prayer chorus on the piano. When we lifted our heads, all the money was gone. The soldiers had come and received the blessing. Now we would all wait and see what God would do.

During that next week, people stopped us to say they had taken money to buy the supplies needed to wash cars, to do some sewing, hair cutting, and other simple tasks that the soldiers would do to gain a return in the name of the Lord. One woman mentioned that she hadn't taken any money but thought she would sell some things she already had to support the cause. Three weeks passed, and as people brought in their offering, the bookkeeper would place it in the safe in a bank deposit bag without counting it. We had committed to opening the bag for the first time to count it before the entire congregation in the Sunday morning Holiness Meeting.

On the Thursday of the last week before the Sunday report, I snuck a peek to see how it was going. Imagine my surprise when I counted all of $78 and change! Carolyn was away that week, and I called to tell her to pray hard for not just a multiplying of the talents, but with "loaves and fishes" faith, if we were going to honor God on Sunday. At home alone, I prayed and fasted for God's blessing.

When Sunday came, I carried the bank bag into the chapel and placed it on the Holiness Table. At the appropriate time in the meeting, I opened it and counted the money. With all the change and dollar bills, it came to exactly $600—double the amount we had placed in faith before the Lord. Unknown to me, one of the men had come by the hall on Saturday, just when the bookkeeper happened to be there, and dropped off some money. He had taken more than $150 at the soldiers meeting to help a neighbor pay his family's home heating bill. On Saturday the neighbor gave him a bag of uncounted cash in gratitude for the help. After that Sunday, the corps' financial pressures simply went away. It was a miracle.

4. What's the best innovation you've helped create or extend?

There have been many imaginative endeavors over the years … almost too many to count. I think the People Count and 210 in 2010 campaigns are strong candidates, as was the Soup's On program in Philadelphia, a program that paid a living wage as people went through advanced culinary training.

In the corps in Wilkes–Barre, Pennsylvania, we launched two initiatives, S.A.V.E. and L.O.V.E—Salvation Army Video Evangelism and Local Officer Visitation Evangelism. This was just when video cameras and players were first being marketed to the public. We borrowed a large player/recorder about the size of a microwave machine and twice as heavy. We recorded our Holiness Meetings and visited people who couldn't get to the meeting with the equipment and videotapes. The visit always drew the whole family crowd because the homes didn't have video players yet, so it was quite a special opportunity. We carried Salvation Army songbooks because the families wanted to sing all the songs and even stand as they would in the meeting. They even passed a hat for the offering. As a result, the local officers were motivated by love to increase their visitation, which encouraged many to come back to the corps and join in the ministries.

5. What's the best means of influence and how have you used it?

Prayer.

COMMISSIONER JAMES KNAGGS, and his wife, Commissioner Carolyn Knaggs, had served their whole officership in their home territory, USA East, when they were appointed to lead the Australia Southern Territory. They served there for four years before heading up the USA Western Territory.

Throughout his active service, Commissioner Knaggs has emphasized evangelism and corps planting, engaging in aggressive evangelistic campaigns from his cadet days through to ambitious corps growth campaigns as territorial commander. He is known for his standby exhortation, "Be holy and show up for work."

STAY—AND CHANGE THINGS

LT. COLONEL MIRIAM GLUYAS

1. What is the best thing about being a Salvation Army officer?

I feel like I was born to be a Salvation Army officer. I love the fact that I get to be in relationship with Jesus, that I get to spend time with Him every day, and that I get to partner up with Him in seeing His Kingdom come and His will be done. There's nothing better than that.

For me, the best things about being a Salvation Army officer are (a) seeing God at work and (b) people.

When I was stationed at Auburn Corps, a lady came to welfare. The person ministering to her that day recognized that she needed more than a food parcel. Because of the difficulties in her life and the life of her daughter who lived with her, the Department of Community Services was about to move in and take the children from her and her daughter.

The welfare worker asked a group of our young adults, who were keen about doing acts of kindness, to help this family. That group of passionate young Christians went around to the house; they cleaned up, painted, mowed the lawns, and did everything they could to sort the place out. At the end of the day that lady said, "If that's what your Jesus is like, I want to get to know Him."

The issue of the children needed to be dealt with, and we needed a solicitor [attorney] to help out. One of the young adults asked a favor of a friend named Luke, a rather clued-in solicitor. Luke turned up and represented the family. We asked him to come along to church, where we celebrated him ... and asked him to help us with another case. Luke and the lady kept on coming. Both became passionate about Jesus.

Luke then felt that God was telling him to start up what is now known as Courtyard Legal. Every Monday night he would come to Auburn and serve those in the community who desperately needed legal help but couldn't afford it. He brought with him many solicitors and lawyers, who did pro bono work. In five years, more than 1,000 people were served. The success rate—in 325 cases—was 97 percent. Refugee families were reunited; people's lives were transformed; the voiceless were given a voice.

Luke later left a partnership in a firm to work full time for the Salvos. God has given him so many dreams, and they are becoming realities. There is a strong calling on his life. He lives to serve those who need help and need Jesus.

One of the delights of officership is seeing people rise up and shine, seeing their lives transformed by Jesus, and seeing them partner up with Him to change this world. To have any part in that is an incredible privilege.

What if we hadn't trained up our people for mission? What if the welfare worker on duty that day hadn't recognized a deeper need? What if those young people weren't passionate about acts of kindness and sharing Jesus? What if we hadn't invited a young solicitor to help us, celebrated him, and invited him back? What if lives were not transformed by Jesus?

No "what ifs" in this story. God did an amazing work in and through

His people. And that continues on. What a privilege.

2. What keeps you in officership when things are tough?

There is no doubt that things get tough. I would say that my best and worst times have been had while I've been an officer. We're in a battle. The devil hates it when God's at work. I expect the battle. But I know who has already won the victory! That makes a difference.

There are three key things that keep me in officership when things get tough:

- Calling
- There's nothing I would rather do.
- Believing that we are in urgent and exciting days.

First, the call. I wasn't someone who struggled with a call to officership. I had plans to be a sports teacher and professional golfer. God had plans for me to be a Salvation Army officer; God called me, and I knew that was what I was to do with my life; and I have no regrets at all.

There have been many difficult times in officership, but very few times when I have seriously considered giving up. Once or twice, when I've been frustrated and annoyed, it's probably crossed my mind: "God, are you sure you don't want me to serve in another ministry?" The answer has come immediately: "No, you will stay, and you will change things." Nice!

I'm called. I'm called to The Salvation Army ... and that calling keeps me.

Second, there is nothing I would rather do. No one has to tell me to get up every day and go to work. I know how God has wired me, and what He has wired me for.

I am passionate about: (1) Him; (2) seeing His Kingdom grow; (3)

seeing The Salvation Army grow; (4) seeing leaders develop; (5) justice; (6) the next generation; (7) multicultural ministry. I have annoying days and frustrating days, but the call of God is very real, and I'm passionate about Him and his Kingdom.

Third, I believe absolutely that we are in urgent and exciting days. The world needs Jesus. As I go through the day I think, *How can we see everyone we meet come to experience this magnificent relationship with Jesus? How do we touch lives for Him? How do we become part of people's lives?* I'm not content with the way things are, and that's a good thing. We're also in exciting days. God is touching lives; He is changing lives. He still has a place for His Salvation Army.

So ... who would want to miss out on that?

3. What is the greatest move of God you have experienced in an appointment?

I have experienced two great moves of God. They came, I believe, because of a defining day in my life.

I had just moved into my new appointment at Eastlakes, a church plant in Newcastle. God very clearly said to me, "So are you going to do it your way or My way this time?" Pretty rude, I thought! But I knew what God was saying. I had done things very much in my own strength before this. From that point on, I would start each day saying, "God, I can't, but You can."

At Eastlakes, we fasted and prayed and saw so many miracles.

- God provided leaders for us. We didn't have money for a men's pastor and needed around $17,000 to make that happen. Someone came to see me one day to give us some money. He didn't know what we were praying for, but guess how much he gave us? $17,000.
- Most weeks, people got saved, and they couldn't wait to tell

their friends and family about Jesus. Our church grew
through friendship evangelism.

- We saw God grow a church plant from nothing to a thriving,
healthy corps.

God then sent me to a corps that was 110 years old. In the weeks
before I arrived there, He gave me a vision of what might be, and the
unfolding of that vision continues today and will for years and years
to come.

Auburn was a lovely corps, a corps with every generation, a corps
with incredibly kind and good people, a very Anglo corps, sitting in
the middle of one of the most multicultural areas of Sydney. Central
to that area is a huge mosque.

We started to see things with the eyes of Jesus. We workshopped
who we were, what we wanted to be, what God was saying, how
we would get there. We prayed and believed and partnered up with
God.

- We held Kids Club in the local park, organized soccer games,
served halal sausages, and shared Jesus.
- We opened a drop-in center for the community.
- Some of our soldiers became advocates for people who were
treated unfairly.
- Courtyard Legal started. We saw the voiceless gain a voice,
refugee families reunited, people in trouble with the law
offered hope.

And God brought the nations to us.

- We welcomed refugees at the airport, gave them food parcels,
taught them the basics of life in Australia.
- We ran English conversation classes.

- Some of our people provided homework help to refugee children.
- Each time someone from another country came, we would put that person's national flag up in the hall.

People were saved most weeks. And we enjoyed the favor of our community.

We simply prayed, tried to see our community through God's eyes, tried to see where He was at work, then partnered up with Him. We saw God transforming our community and transforming our entire church. We learned to love our community and love our church.

4. What's the best innovation you've helped to create or extend?

God is amazingly creative. He's always at work. We really do need to seek Him and see what it is He wants to do.

Auburn and Eastlakes are totally different places. Eastlakes is near Newcastle, north of Sydney. At the time I was there, it was about 96 percent Anglo-Saxon. Auburn is in the middle of a very multicultural community. But what I love is that God had, and still has, His plan for both of those places. Both grew incredibly. In both places we saw so many salvations, so many lives transformed, so many people loved and served, the community impacted by Jesus. And it continues on. Very different plans for the two places, but He is key, and transformation is key.

I still constantly ask God, "What's next?" I love that part of officership. I love that part of life. I've never felt like the Army has stopped me from doing anything. Some people may have been nervous at times, but I just want to be careful that anything new is very much of Him.

5. What's the best means of influence and how have you used it?

Leadership is certainly about influence. It's certainly about having followers. It's certainly about investing in the lives of people.

A lot of my time is spent one-on-one with people. I believe very strongly in raising leaders and coaching and mentoring. God has put something in me to be a "potential see-er." He shows me people He wants to use and asks me to see the best in them, see what they could become, and help them to get there. It's really a matter of "raise them up and let them shine."

I have around a dozen people I catch up with on a monthly basis, for an hour a month, and I work with them in the areas of mentoring and coaching. Having sought God, I speak into people the best that I see for them. If God talks to me about their future, I'll talk to them about that, always being careful that they have others praying and confirming things for them.

I also believe that we work best in the body of Christ when we work as teams, bringing the best people around us. There is no place for being threatened by others.

When I went to Auburn, I also had another role in the territory, so I needed a young couple to work with me. I knew that Nesan and Cheryl Kistan had gifts I would never have, gifts that would be valuable for the Kingdom. We gathered a team around us, people with all kinds of different personalities and giftings. We sowed into them, gave them the resources that they needed, and let them shine. Now that's a great delight.

I also believe strongly in the power of vision. People will sign up to a big vision. They want to be part of something that is bigger than them. They also need the chance to dream, to express that dream and have it taken seriously. The vision must be of God if is to become a reality. If it is of God, it's bigger than us.

These are exciting days! We have a magnificent God. We have some wonderful people. We are believing together that His Kingdom will come and that His will will be done!

LT. COLONEL MIRIAM GLUYAS, from the Australia Eastern Territory, is chief secretary in the Papua New Guinea Territory. She has been closely associated with innovative and faith–filled initiatives and has intentionally replicated herself in potential leaders through discipleship and mentoring relationships.

PARTNERING WITH GOD

MAJOR BRYCE DAVIES

1. What is the best thing about being a Salvation Army officer?

I am positioned with a strategic advantage to connect with and impact the poor and marginalized. I have the time, training, and resources to come alongside with help such as a meal and a place to stay, but also the opportunity to show God's love in ways that bring hope and transformation. Few people trust anyone more with this journey than they do a Salvo officer. This enables me to follow the way of Jesus within a very supportive framework.

2. What keeps you in officership when things are tough?

I am a great believer in weekly Sabbath and the power of nourishing a genuinely humble spirit. God is the creator and sustainer of all things; I am very small and needy. This relationship of dependence is vital when times get tough. Only then can the hope and capacity for selfless service, despite the worldly circumstances, have any longevity.

I once was on a four-day silent retreat and felt led to climb a nearby mountain. The context of this experience was that I felt totally inadequate for the task set before me in my ministry. I was angry with God for setting me up to fail. I had been obedient, but He had let me walk straight into trouble and challenges beyond my capacity. As I walked, I was aware of God's presence, and I was seeking His guidance and reassurance. The mountain was big, and after two hours of uphill climbing through uncharted bush I found myself exhausted, scratched, and bruised. Confronted by a sheer wall of rock with no way up, I cried out loud to God, "This is too hard. I can't go on unless you help me!"

This was the cry of my heart in ministry as well as in the physical climb. I had no way to go forward that I could see, but "by faith," I started to ascend by a route that seemed clearly pointless. As I climbed a meter or two, I was given a different view of the cliff face than I had had from the lower position. From here I could see a path up that had previously been hidden—with steps and everything. I climbed with ease and, on reaching the top, found myself with hands raised and voice lifted high praising God for His very specific and wonderful reassurance in my life. No amount of counseling or logic could have encouraged me in spirit as this experience did at that time.

3. What is the greatest move of God you have experienced in an appointment?

My current appointment at Brisbane Street Level Mission is an amazing work of God. Meeting in a garage in a side street in one of the most troubled areas of Brisbane, we have consistently had more than 50 in our chapel service, a spirit of worship that most established corps would kill for, and a desire for membership and commitment like I have never experienced. In six months of ministry we enrolled 12 adherents, all new to faith and the Army. We have a culture of service and grace toward others that is heartwarming and, in our raw but sincere recruits, a zeal for growth and saving the lost that is effective and clearly empowered by God's Spirit.

Recently an alcoholic we have loved and embraced in our community, but who was currently in the middle of a massive bender, rang me and expressed his desire to get into detox. I was off site and unavailable at the time of his call, so I contacted some of our volunteers to act on this opportunity. They shared with me how, when I rang, they had all just been praying for this fellow and discussing how best to intervene in his life.

This kind of scenario is repeated on a regular basis in this appointment and creates excitement and meaning. We are partnering with God. He hears the cries of the poor. We listen to the Spirit and act as His body under the direction of the Head. We are the very hands and feet of Christ, and as we experience His supernatural promptings and leadings, we find ourselves in the right place at the right time. Something bigger than all of us is working things out and we have anticipation each day as to how this will be played out—even in our little lives!

4. What's the best innovation you've helped create or extend?

We have operated an espresso coffee van and done festivals and fairs, and all the workers and helpers are people from our street ministry. Many have never held a job and few have good prospects for work due to addiction, mental health problems, and a generally inconsistent lifestyle. But together we can run a coffee van and do a good job. Serving people, taking orders, and making fair-trade coffee provides a meaningful and community-enhancing experience. They all wear Salvo shields with pride and will talk enthusiastically about our community and the great sense of belonging they now experience.

This is a great witness and PR exercise and gives many meaningful opportunities to our people, including training as baristas and café workers. Employment Plus wants to place people on training courses with us. The law courts have considered sentencing people to do community hours on the coffee van.

5. What's the best means of influence and how have you used it?

My best influence is my personal walk with God and the outworking of this in my life.

I come from a family where work and Army were the main priorities and where the integrity of family life became compromised and out of balance. I do not think this is an uncommon scenario within Army circles. An example of my walk with God that challenged this was a decision I made when our children were young to be clearly devoted as a husband and father—even at the expense of ministry and popular opinion. I felt a little ripped off, but trusted God that this was an important season of my life. During this time my marriage relationship improved and my parenting was accompanied by great joy and love for my two girls.

I began to mentor a few young men associated with the local corps in Adelaide, and found them very teachable and warm to my guidance and encouragement. I wondered what seemed to attract these young guys to me as a mentor, as I am no scholar, not even a great counselor. The response was that they saw in me a love for my wife and kids that they wanted and needed to learn about. This—not ministry skills or innovative approaches—was the appealing aspect. God has used these young guys in ministry, and I count those years of mentoring as some of the most fruitful and influential of my officership.

MAJOR BRYCE DAVIES serves at Brisbane Street Level Mission in Australia Eastern, his home territory. From his early years Bryce embraced the banding and youth activities of The Salvation Army. He entered training college after having learned a trade as a plumber and running his own successful business. As an officer, he has been heavily involved in addiction and homeless programs. He lives in Brisbane with wife, Major Sue Davies, and has two daughters, Eliza and Georgia. The family has also lived in Melbourne and Adelaide.

AN OPPORTUNITY TO GIVE BACK

LT COLONEL EDDIE HOBGOOD

1. What is the best thing about being a Salvation Army officer?

For me, it's the opportunity to give back.

When I was born, I was given up by my birth mother, so I grew up feeling unwanted. Of course, in a kid's mind, for the woman who gave me birth to give me away, either there had to be something wrong with me or I had done something really bad that caused her to stop loving me. Even though I was adopted, this knowledge haunted me, and I felt that I was totally unworthy of anyone's love.

As a preteen, I found the Army—or, rather, the Army found me. I was unconditionally accepted and loved, which mirrored Christ's love for me. It totally changed and transformed me. I knew God was calling me to officership. He kept bringing back to my mind how this would be an opportunity for me to have the same kind of ministry to others that was transformational in my own life.

2. What keeps you in officership when things are tough?

Every time things have gotten tough, someone has sent me a card, phoned me up, or dropped by to visit and offer me encouragement.

Not long ago, my schedule had become too full. I had overcommitted myself and was feeling the stress and pressure of not having enough time to prepare and the physical toll of stretching myself too thin. Then an email popped up on my screen from a young man who had worked for me when I was a corps officer. I had been away from that appointment for over 10 years, and we had sporadically exchanged emails. For whatever reason, he wrote me that day to share with me about how influential I had been in his life. He said he was involved in ministry today because of the godliness he had seen in me and the example of Jesus that I had shown him during our three years of working together.

I was blown away, moved to tears and grateful that God had given me the opportunity to be a blessing to this great young man. It's those kinds of moments that reaffirm the calling God placed on my life.

3. What is the greatest move of God you have experienced in an appointment?

It was at a territorial youth gathering when I was TYS. One of our young men had been tragically killed in a car accident. There was a huge cloud over the entire event. Everyone was trying to deal with the loss, especially his girlfriend, who was about to become his fiancée. One morning during our worship time, the young lady just collapsed on the floor, crying hysterically. Everything stopped as people surrounded her and began to pray. Then others who were experiencing difficulties moved to the front to pray. Still others began to form small groups and sing softly and pray.

I don't remember how much time passed—it seemed like an eternity and it seemed like a moment. God the Holy Spirit fell on that room and moved in a way I had never seen before in a Salvation Army meeting. I had read about it in Army history books but never witnessed it. Before we knew it, it was lunchtime and we had been praying and worshiping and singing for over three hours! Slowly, people began to leave, but quite a few stayed and continued to pray.

This was the third day of a week-long event. Most of the morning sessions never happened that week because that scene was repeated almost every day. It was one of the most amazing and spiritually significant events of my life!

4. What's the best innovation you've helped create or extend?

At the youth event just described, the worship was incredible. Most of the kids went back home to corps that had little or no music and certainly nothing contemporary. So we took the worship band that had led us at the event and recorded a CD called *Send the Fire*. It became the #1 worship CD produced by the Army and to this day, although we've produced six or eight more, it is still by far the most used.

During the time I was TYS, we also produced a cartoon video called *Captain Gabriel versus the League of Darkness*. It was aimed at teaching junior soldiers that they all have a part to play in the fight against sin and injustice in the world. We produced it in Spanish at the same time, and when I was in Chile recently doing earthquake relief, I met some corps officers who recognized my name because of the cartoon. They said it was a huge hit and a popular teaching resource in their corps! Who would have ever thought that little cartoon would make it to some obscure town in Chile!

5. What's the best means of influence and how have you used it?

Theater has played a huge part in my life. Growing up extremely poor and in a very depressed area, my escape was theater. When I became an officer, I thought I would have to give up any dreams I had of doing anything theatrical. Boy, was I wrong! From Day One, I have been able to blend my love of theater with my love of ministry.

I created a one-man presentation based on one of the most radical

Salvationists ever, Joe the Turk. God has given me the opportunity to present it all across North America, as well as in Argentina and the United Kingdom.

More recently I was commissioned to write a musical about the life of Commissioner Samuel Logan Brengle. It premiered at the Southern Territorial Holiness Congress to an audience of 7,000. It went on to be presented at the International Leaders Conference at Sunbury Court in London for all the top leadership of the worldwide Army and at the World Youth Conference in Stockholm. The USA Eastern Territory and the Barbados Division have produced versions of the musical as well.

I'm extremely grateful to God for taking this offering and using it in ways beyond my wildest imagination. A soundtrack CD and a DVD of the original cast production have been produced and sent out across the world. I continually get emails from people who tell me that something in the musical ministered to them at a critical moment in their lives. Praise God!

I'm blown away by all this, but I shouldn't be surprised. This project was bathed in prayer. While I was writing it, not a day went by that I didn't hear from someone telling me they were praying for me specifically while I wrote. I never felt stress, just total peace about the project and an overwhelming sense of God's presence with each word that I typed or note that I penned.

LT. COLONEL EDDIE HOBGOOD, from the USA Southern Territory, was appointed coordinator for the International Congress in London in July 2015. A first–generation Salvationist, he is known as an initiator and innovator. With a bilingual (English and Spanish) background, Colonel Hobgood has invested in the Salvation War on Spanish–speaking fronts in the Americas. He is well known for creating and presenting plays on Joe the Turk, Samuel Logan Brengle, and William and Catherine Booth.

ARISE AND MAKE HISTORY

MAJOR IVAN BEZZANT

1. What is the best thing about being a Salvation Army officer?

Imagine God planting a work that will be significant in restoring His Kingdom here on Earth. In this work His intention is to make and release radical disciples. The focus of this work is the nations, to influence business, education, the family, arts, entertainment, sports, science and medicine, government—both local and central—media, and, yes, even the Church. The focus is the restoration of His Kingdom rule, His government, in these nations. For 150 years, He has led, directed, provided, and empowered.

Now consider God looking out upon creation and choosing leaders of leaders to lead this work—and He chooses you. Wow! God knows all about your weaknesses, yet He calls you to lead in this great endeavor for His Kingdom. This must be the best thing about being a Salvation Army officer. To join in this mission along with your spiritual ancestors who have carried the vision, to honor their part in the journey, and now to take hold of your moment in history and live with eyes on the past, serving the present, and reaching into the future to pass on to the next generation of officers the mantle of leadership of this great work.

For me, this is the best thing about being a Salvation Army officer. To wake up each day knowing that you are part of a great work and your work is not in vain. To know you belong to something bigger than you. To arise and make history.

2. What keeps you in officership when things are tough?

It's imperative to know you have been called. As a cadet, I visited a retired officer who gave me some wisdom that has helped me through the years. He spoke about pursuing a clear understanding of my calling. He said I needed to nail the call of God upon my life for officership. He said there would be times when I would have lists of reasons to leave and there would be only one reason to stay. That would be: "God has called me."

This may seem corny to some. It may sound "too spiritual" to others. The reality for me is this: I believe that because I am God's son it is possible for me to hear His voice clearly on this matter.

Building on this foundation stone of knowing the call, I face life knowing storms will come. Storms will reveal the character of what I have been building, what is really going on internally. So I embrace the tough times, understanding that God is still in control, He knew all about this. My faith must rest in the knowledge that I will go through and come from this experience made more into His likeness.

Again, when I was a cadet, a senior officer told me a principle he held onto through the tough times in his officership: "It shall come to pass." He encouraged me to make this a statement I would say to myself in times of trouble. I have practiced this and found it to be true. It has comforted me in times of difficulty. It was a statement of hope when I could not see anything but trouble and became a word of testimony as I exited the time of trouble a better person and a better leader.

An example of this has been in financing the work we have pursued, which carries a cost that always seems impossible to meet. I find it to be very stressful when it appears that we will not be able to meet budgets or expectations. In those times, I turn again in faith to understanding God's call upon my life and announce, "It shall come to pass." Then I trust in God to provide for the work He has called into being.

3. What is the greatest move of God you have experienced in an appointment?

The work of God over a period of 10 years in the Napier Corps, New Zealand.

- God providing facilities that in human eyes were impossible. The building of a work far greater than could be accounted for given the financial resources at hand.
- Experiencing the Holy Spirit in revival, empowering His people to know their God and behold the miracles of God. Seeing people healed, physically and spiritually. Seeing dysfunctional people become active, alive, significant, and growing into wholeness.
- Within the corps, seeing God build relationships between people and bring about an awesome level of community.
- God's people catching a vision of what God can do through their lives as they submit to Him and thus bring transformation and influence to the city. Hearing the mayor tell me that the city council had agreed that The Salvation Army is a growth industry in the city.
- Becoming an influence in the nation. Modeling a Kingdom lifestyle that attracts people to change.

It's all about God moving! About God being God.

4. What's the best innovation you've helped create or extend?

A number of years ago, I was challenged by a senior officer to create a training module focusing on what I believe are keys to developing leaders. From this challenge came Leadership Jesus' Way. Later, in response to our territory's strategic plan for growth, Leadership Jesus' Way became a resource for the territory to use to train in discipleship and leadership. A Discipleship School has emerged, and we now have students around the country who are part of this school. Leadership Jesus' Way has opened doors of ministry in coaching and mentoring. I am amazed at how God has used this material.

5. What's the best means of influence and how have you used it?

Staying teachable and allowing God to train you so that the message you present is lived out in you in such a way that you carry authority. Being faithful to what I call key life messages, messages God has given you that have brought transformation. We understand from the life of Christ that change comes about not from presenting His Word alone, but there needs to be a transfer of this life as the Word becomes incarnate. Influence comes as you are able to carry life that is then passed on to others.

I am convinced that what this world needs today are spiritual mothers and fathers, leaders who will live a life that calls others to follow. Over the years it has been my privilege to have people come and ask to spend time with me as they saw in me a lifestyle they wanted to pursue for themselves.

MAJOR IVAN BEZZANT, now divisional commander of the Southern Division of his home territory, New Zealand, Fiji, and Tonga, has spent most of his officership in corps appointments. He and his wife, Major Glenda Bezzant, have two adult children who are married and serving as committed disciples and soldiers of The Salvation Army. Ivan has run Leadership Jesus' Way Conferences around New Zealand and is a passionate believer that the best days of the Salvation Army are to come. His life mission is to raise an army that will make a difference in the midst of the battle. He carries a burden for revival and believes we were created to invade the impossible.

'AREN'T YOU GLAD YOU JOINED?' SURE AM.

COLONEL MARGARET HAY

1. What is the best thing about being a Salvation Army officer?

Access into settings and lives beyond my imagining. The sense of "this grace in which we stand" (Romans 5:2 ESV) as the springboard first struck me on hearing my father, Elliott Major, sometimes needing air from in-house pressures at the corps, saying to my mother: "Greta, where's my harness [his uniform] and the *Cry's*, I'm off down to the pub to meet some sane people!" It continued when as a 20-something officer freshly arrived in Zambia I breathed with relief at the welcome by a revered Zambian comrade quoting the proverb: "The visitor also helped in the battle."

And it's been a recurrent theme right through, lived out in a stream of fellow officers, like Major Suresh Pawar of the India Western Territory, who summed up our business by saying: "We need to cling to the truth that God has won victory for His people on the Cross, and the enemy is already defeated. And we need to live amongst the people, feel what they feel, and together be able to see the abundance of God's grace."

2. What keeps you in officership when things are tough?

My active officership, from the 1960s to the 2000s, straddled the era when the lives of married women officers were revolutionized, with a role change from supporter, wife, mother, to holding independent appointments. I found myself catapulted from having no specific responsibility, expending my energy on anxiety for those closest to me, into active roles—some a pure pleasure, others with administrative demands beyond my knowledge and experience.

Rough patches in the ride were negotiated by drawing on my strong sense of calling, and of being in good company. In some rigorous moments I heard the voice of the Lord urging: "It's going to be all right." And there have been plenty of laughs and larks as well, and great comrades, like Canada's Commissioner John Nelson in the thick of ventures in Asia booming, "Aren't you glad you joined?" Sure am.

3. What is the greatest move of God you have experienced in an appointment?

I've been startled lots of times by seeing the movement of God, especially in places where things are badly broken. A famous commissioner, A.J. Gilliard, who as New Zealand territorial commander in the early 1960s impacted many of us students of that day, was a passionate internationalist. He wrote of "the early days, when William Booth's young men and women went like a swift ocean wave out into the unknown, there to touch young men and women of other races and cultures in the glory of Pentecostal brotherhood." Gilliard saw that this vision, distantly glimpsed in the time of the Founder, would find increasing depth and enrichment by the contributions of Salvationists of many nations.

Wide-eyed, I saw the power of that visionary wave while working with asylum seekers at HM Prison Rochester in Kent, England. In my first week there in 1999, I entered a wing and was immediately surrounded by a large group of young men from the former Yugoslavia who, with the war over, had fled to England with hopes of safe haven and work, only to find themselves arrested at the border and held in prison conditions. None would have known The Salvation Army, but the sight of the unfamiliar uniform might mean some help was at hand. Then I heard the blessed words "Salvation Army!" from the upper floor of the wing. It was a Nigerian detainee, who called out that he had attended Army schools. Next minute he was down among the young Balkans, vigorously explaining that The Salvation Army is a Christian church, that these people are good, and that the Army can do anything!

I saw the "Pentecostal brotherhood" again breathtakingly at work a few years later when, with a group of delegates to the International College for Officers (ICO), I led a service at the Rochester prison. The best part was at the end, when inmates met the group of officers who represented half a dozen languages. The sight that still raises the hair on my neck was of Major Alex Kharkov, his face alight, surrounded by a group of desperate men from Russia, China, and a cluster of remote Central European states. "They shall come from the east" indeed: Gilliard's vision of the unlimited potential of our international calling exemplified.

The same international wave is experienced with force by anyone at the ICO, spending evenings sitting close as privileged listeners to a tide of testimony. For me it's typified by the memory of an American officer on his knees as he spoke to the group, partly to keep his sturdy frame from blocking the projection screen, but mainly in thanksgiving to God for his salvation and calling as he recalled a chilling childhood, then conscription to the Vietnam War as a last–ditch alternative to prison, a life almost on the scrapheap—almost, but for amazing grace.

And there are streams of other memories: How about Major Eva

Kleman emailing during a freezing February in Sweden to tell of a turnaround in her husband Johnny's health, which enabled them to take up new appointments in Finland? Eva wrote: "It's a kind of spring experience when you feel that things are going in the right direction. We are so happy. We have learned the hard lesson to take one day at a time, and at the same time it is a blessing not taking everything for granted. Life becomes a great—super—wonderful thing!" How irresistible is such deep and subversive faith in the Resurrection at work.

4. What's the best innovation you've helped create or extend?

In the past decade I've been changed through involvement in integrated mission in places facing a tsunami of challenges. The access idea lurched from rhetoric to reality as I sat in a tiny house in Mumbai and watched a dynamic encounter among four colleagues, three of them local, and a woman being served by the Army's Community-Based Aids Program. It's about facing the awkwardness of encounter, about listening, about engagement in a relationship that changes all involved. It's about hope, a realistic hope that searches for real possibilities, the acid test always being: Does it work in the back streets?

Home in New Zealand in the early stages of retirement, I'm both proud and prodded by the Spirit as I look forward. The pride comes from this territory's sustained commitment to taking significant steps to eradicate poverty, through impressive, rigorously researched engagement with government, along with streetwise, grassroots involvement in corps and centers up and down the land.

The prodding concerns the needed learning and increasing immersion in enterprises, local, national, and even global, as the Spirit says, "Do!"

5. What's the best means of influence, and how have you used it?

I was startled in the year 2000 to be awarded the accolade of Preacher of the Year by *The Times* of London. The winning sermon was prepared on the passage from Isaiah 9: "The people who walked in darkness have seen a great light" (ESV)—the set text on the very day that a young inmate in Brixton prison, London, peering in the semi-darkness through the bars of his cell door, had asked, "What time is it, Miss, what day is it?"

The intersection of the Word and the world that resulted from *The Times* award hugely increased my influence and the challenges that went with it. I, who had never taught a course in homiletics, found myself coming home from the prison day after day and giving interviews face-to-face, then down the line in England and far beyond. And I was invited to preach in some astounding venues, the privilege magnified by the lectionary texts: the Transfiguration in Salisbury Cathedral, the Prodigal Son at Winchester, and, in Westminster Abbey, the Conversion of St. Paul. To God, the One who takes the weak and foolish things and uses them to His glory, be the praise.

And still no privilege could be greater than to stand close in a grim little prison room with a group of fellow believers, asylum-seekers, at a weekly Bible study and to hear the words of the Grace, always ending there with "and the sweet fellowship of the Holy Spirit be with you."

It's the access thing: involvement with people, and then in preaching to trace and voice, as Walter Brueggemann says, "the delicate, tortured, dramatic way in which God moves us from one world to the other... a new truth-filled world in which people may come to live again with the freedom that belongs peculiarly to God's children." Which is why my constant prayer has been and is:

Jesus, confirm my heart's desire
To work and think and speak for thee;
Still let me guard the holy fire,
And still stir up thy gift in me.

Charles Wesley (*SASB*, 199)

COLONEL MARGARET HAY, M.B.E., M.A., DIP.TCHG., DIP.TESL., has served in corps and educational centers in Zambia, Hong Kong, and the UK, as well as in her home territory, New Zealand, Fiji, and Tonga. She has been principal of Salvation Army officer training colleges in Hong Kong and New Zealand and of the International College for Officers, London. In 2000, while serving as a chaplain and foreign nationals coordinator for detained asylum seekers at HM Prison Rochester, UK, she was honored to become *The Times* of London Preacher of the Year. She is married to Laurence, has four grown children, and lives in retirement in a small township in the south of New Zealand.

A SIPIRT OF HUMILITY

LT. COLONEL TIMOTHY MABASO

1. What is the best thing about being a Salvation Army officer?

It is of vital importance to start by pointing out that to me being an officer is a divine call from God rather than a career. God did not speak to me as he spoke to Abraham, Moses, David, or Jeremiah, all of whom were great men of the Bible. Yet He spoke and called me from where I was, challenging me by the needs of the people I lived with every day—many of whom were my peers. I answered the call to become a Salvation Army officer after I was convicted by the Holy Spirit that I would become an instrument through which God could speak to and with His people.

The best thing about being a Salvation Army officer, for me, is the privilege to serve God's people through The Salvation Army. I cherish, with humility, the fact that I am able to touch people's lives and claim, with the granted authority, the blessings of Jesus Christ.

Being a Salvation Army officer is the best thing that I could ever have been in that I have so many avenues of service to God. I preach and teach God's Word. I have the privilege of being God's spokesperson. I feel humbled that God called and entrusted His Word to me for sharing with His people. I use the word "with" deliberately, because I do not believe that God called me only to speak "to" His people, but to share "with" them.

I am privileged to equip the saints, to converse with the unsaved and show the way towards true repentance, and to serve the poor and the marginalized without being judgmental. I can pray and give assurance to the soldiers of The Salvation Army—and other Christians as well—that God does listen to His people. I am called to be a steward of God's Kingdom resources—people being an important part of those resources. I am aware of the great expectation for me to be responsible and accountable with all that God has entrusted to me.

As a Salvation Army officer I am convinced that I have the freedom to be who I am in the Lord, in total reliance on the Holy Spirit's prompting, guidance, and counsel.

Scripture references: Matthew 4:18–22; Mark 10:41–45; Acts 1:8

2. What keeps you in officership when things are tough?

There is no place in the world that does not have its own difficulties and challenges. Problems and tough times are encountered everywhere. I guess that is why we have the saying, "When the going gets tough, the tough get going!" Well, I must confess that I am not a "tough" one, not at all. When things get tough, I rely wholly on the Holy Spirit to keep me going.

It is not only the fact that I signed the covenant that keeps me in officership. It is the constant assurance, and the experience I have had, that God's loving and caring grace is always with me.

Officership has not been a smooth-sailing experience for me. I have been in appointments where it seemed that everyone was against me and those who initiated the move seemed not to care. I felt like I had been thrown into the den of invisible "lions." I have been in appointments where I felt I was not able to utilize my gifts and talents to the utmost. And I have been in situations where I was unable to meet the basic needs of my God-given family. God blessed us with four children—

and it has been tough to take them through school and into institutions of higher learning. For many years I cried when it was time to pay for my children's education and there was no source of income.

I should mention that some of the tough times I have experienced were of my own making. On some occasions I have misjudged a situation and made bad decisions—even terrible mistakes—that created difficulties for the appointment and my officership. On some occasions I have unknowingly undermined those I was appointed to lead, turning what could have been an easy task into a very tough one.

However, in all of this, the Lord's mighty hand has pulled me through. When things were tough, I always found myself in a confrontational conversation with God, and there would always be an answer—sometimes not to my satisfaction, but it always turned out to be a positive answer. When the tough times were of my own making, I turned to God to seek His forgiveness and counsel. God has always been faithful and trustworthy. I have found that in every tough situation there is something or someone to represent God, and I have learned to count my blessings. It is my total dependence on the leadership, protection, and provision of the Holy Spirit that keeps me going when things gets tough.

Officership does not guarantee me an easy life in the world. Officership does not mean I am immune from making mistakes. Officership does not mean I am certain of what the future will be. But one thing I am certain of: the One who has called me will not let me face tough situations alone.

Scripture references: Matthew 6:25–34; Matthew 11:28–30; Philippians 4:10–13

3. What is the greatest move of God you have experienced in an appointment?

I have experienced seemingly unbelievable, wonderful works of God in some of my appointments. I will give two examples.

At one of our appointments, my wife and I were walking within the community doing our regular house-to-house visitation of our soldiers. Obviously we targeted the Salvationists' homes only. We were walking past a house when suddenly, a woman and her husband, recognizing our uniform, greeted us—as it is the African custom to greet people, even strangers—and asked us to come into their house to pray for their grandchild. On going in, we found a young girl of about 8 years lying motionless on a mat. Apparently she had been discharged from hospital seven days before and had been lying on that mat drinking only water and milk. I knelt beside her and prayed—not for healing in particular, but for God's will to be done and for the parents to be blessed through her life. I kind of offered a prayer dedicating the young girl to God. As I finished I had a sense that the parents had expected a different kind of prayer. We left and went on about our plan for the day.

The following day, very early in the morning, there was a knock on our door. It was that non-Salvationist couple whose child we had prayed for. The child was alive, had left the mat, and was playing with her peers! She has grown to be a medical doctor today. That was a move of God! I did not claim "healing powers." I simply accepted that God had answered the prayers of His servants at a time of need.

On another occasion my wife and I were sitting in our quarters not knowing where the next plate of food on our table was to come from. Our children had gone to school hungry that day, and they would come back that afternoon to be offered only a cup of warm water with sugar. My wife and I were not even talking to each other; I was doing some writing, and she was busy preparing for her next women's ministries engagement. Just about an hour before the children were to come home, there was a knock on the door. It was an elderly woman we knew as someone who was despised and marginalized by that community. We were used to hearing only bad stories about her. We had heard that no one greeted her or even visited her house. Well, we welcomed her in and offered her some water. She was carrying a sack full of some stuff.

The woman sat down and told us that she had just been to the pension payout point and felt moved by God to buy something for the officers. We were very reluctant to accept anything from her, based on what we had heard. However, we took her offer in faith. On opening the sack, we found some groceries and some goodies for our two boys. The woman was so happy that we had even dared to welcome her into our house. This was her monthly commitment from then on: each time she went to get her pension she walked past the quarters to leave us something, no matter how small. She later converted to Christianity and became a very strong Salvationist—to the amazement of the members of the community and the Salvationists. That was a move of God.

Scripture references: Mark 11:20-24; Acts 10:1-11:18

4. What's the best innovation you've helped to create or extend?

We were in a corps appointment where the majority of our soldiers were children. There were many programs in which the girls participated, but there was nothing really designed for the boys, apart from singing, playing in the band, or being part of the corps cadet brigade. The boys felt left out. They approached me for some brainstorming. I asked them what they wanted to do about it, and they said to me, "Let's start something like a 'Boys' Beat.'" I thought that was a good idea.

We started a Boys' Beat program that included sports, music, and various other activities as well as teaching, guidance, and prayer. The boys had a saying: "If Christ were to physically join a group, it would have to be the Boys Beat." We also had some common activities for boys and girls together. This program not only impacted our corps community but also had a positive effect on the neighborhood; parents encouraged their children to join us to avoid idleness and drug problems. The Boys' Beat is something that I still thank God for.

In that same corps appointment we had only one man—old enough to be my dad—who attended the services. I decided to initiate a men's fellowship with just the two of us! Then the number grew to four, and within about eight months there were 12 men attending.

We created our own program based on the activities we wanted to engage in and the things we wanted to talk about. As a younger man, I allowed the older men to take the initiative, my role being that of a spiritual guide. Within a year, the fellowship had grown to 18 members and had even attracted some younger men.

It worked wonderfully. Our corps started to see more men not only attending the services but also taking some responsibilities in the operation of the corps. It is amazing what God can do through men who are committed to listening to God's counsel. This strengthened my role and the influence I had as a Salvation Army officer.

Scripture references: 1 Timothy 4:11–5:2; John 10:14–16

5. What's the best means of influence and how have you used it?

I believe that I influence people effectively when I am humble before God. Humility helps me realize that as much as I am an ordained minister of the Gospel of Jesus Christ, I am still a human being who has been saved through, and constantly in need of, the grace of God. In my humility I do not have to feel intimidated or threatened. I believe that humility has increased my ability to become teachable and approachable. Humility has helped me to be obedient before God and be vulnerable to Him in order to lead His people effectively. Humility, to me, a Salvation Army officer, is a spiritual means of influence rather than a professional practice.

Humility makes me accept God's people irrespective of their status or otherwise. It has helped me to regard all of my officer colleagues with the same spirit and treat them equally irrespective of their appointments or mine. In humility I have been able to reach out and build quality relationships with people of all ages.

I was born, and still live, in a country that is rich in diversity of cultures and traditions. The spirit of humility helps me to build bridges, helping God's people to live together in harmony, to embrace and celebrate their diversity.

Humility is my personal commitment and part of my daily conversation with God. It is very challenging to keep on reminding myself of the need to be humble, but it is worth the effort. I am always praying and striving for the "same attitude that Christ Jesus had" (Philippians 2:5 NLT). For it is only then, I believe, that I will be efficient and effective as a Salvation Army officer.

Scripture references: Philippians 2:5-11; 1 Peter 5:1-11; John 13:1-17

LT. COLONEL JEQEZA TIMOTHY MABASO and his wife, Lt. Colonel Ntombi-zakithi Mabaso, are corps officers of the Gemiston City Corps in their home territory, Southern Africa. Before answering God's call to full-time service, Colonel Mabaso worked as a teacher and then joined the corporate world in business management/administration. He has participated in the development of South African society during the move towards a "new dispensation in South Africa," as described in a speech by President F.W. DeKlerk in 1990, which led to the ending of apartheid. The Mabasos have been blessed with four sons and four grandchildren.

DEALING WITH THE REAL STUFF

MAJOR KJELL KARLSTEN

1. What is the best thing about being a Salvation Army officer?

I couldn't be happy with just filling my life with anything less than those things that really matter, the truly important things. I find it difficult to produce much interest in things that are nothing more than entertainment for the present moment. For sure, I can watch a good movie—but as I'm doing it, I'm often restless, because it is not for real. It is not the real business. It is not really important.

Being an officer in the Salvation Army gives me the opportunity to spend my time dealing with the real stuff, the most important thing in life: the salvation of children, men, and women.

There is no guarantee that your time is used meaningfully just because you are an officer, but at least you have availed yourself of the best prerequisite. I have worked most of my time as a corps officer but also as divisional youth secretary and territorial youth secretary. In each appointment I have been given opportunities to do what I like best and find most important, fascinating, and inspiring: to teach, train, plan, and lead the troops into the Salvation War.

I am a visionary person and I love to be able to catch a vision for a situation or a place and try to incarnate that. Together with my team, I worked out a vision for Visby and for Gotland, the city and island where we serve. (Gotland is an island in the Baltic Sea.) Believing that God wanted to make this place a center for prayer, we set out to establish a House of Prayer for All People, where prayer is going on 24/7—both a power station and a refuge. We started to pray for "Anna souls" (Luke 2:36-37) to come and work in this House of Prayer.

We started a school, the Saved2Save Training School, to train missionaries, frontline soldiers, for the Salvation War, but we are convinced that we cannot succeed in this war unless we also build a strong and persistent prayer ministry.

These are the things that really inspire me: the hope and the chance to influence my world and to see God's Kingdom come.

2. What keeps you in officership when things are tough?

Being at war is *always* tough—at least in my world! There is constant spiritual pressure and—again, at least in my world—a constant experience of backfire.

I live in what is said to be the most secularized part of the world. The Kingdom of God has not been expanding the way we had hoped for in Sweden or in Europe as a whole during the last decades—rather the opposite. Being in this situation, I find it very helpful to read about and meditate on the lives of heroes of faith, past and present. I try to identify and draw strength from the stories of heroic brothers and sisters around the world. I also gain much strength from meeting brothers and sisters with a similar heart and a similar passion, to pray and to share.

And just relaxing at a nice café reading a good book or a magazine helps me to gain perspective, to realize that God has things under control and that He will finally see His will through with or without me.

3. What is the greatest move of God you have experienced in an appointment?

When I look back on my time in officership, I would have to say that the whole process I have been in is the greatest and most unexpected move of God that I have seen. Direct from officer training, my wife and I were asked if we would be willing to move to Gotland. We agreed. During our time on the island, we worked intensively to reach out to young people, especially in the summer, and the prayer work was just as intense. God brought people together from all the different churches to the Army hall every Friday to pray for the island.

We also experienced strong opposition, such as people in the different churches collecting names on a petition to THQ to remove us from the island because we disturbed the peace and were seen as dangerous. However, we received support from divisional and territorial leaders and remained. During that time God spoke to us about Gotland and gave us a clear understanding of His plan and vision for Visby, the main city of the island. After five years we were given a new appointment and moved away, sensing that we would be back at some point to see what God had spoken to us being fulfilled.

Five years later, the corps on the island had more or less died. Meanwhile, we had become more and more convinced that our calling is of a pioneer nature more than anything else. When we suggested to the Army leadership that we move back to the island to restart the corps, the idea was well received. So, five years later, we were back, and have now been at Gotland for another 21 years.

To serve in the same place for a very long time—more than 25 years—is both very demanding and very rewarding. Gotland is a rough place spiritually, and the corps is still not a large one. We worked mostly with children and young people, and they most often move away from the island as they grow up, for studies and to find a job. Nevertheless, the corps now has a substantial permanent core of people, and we are more and more working out God's calling for His church on the island as well as His plans and purposes for the island itself.

To see a place being transformed by God is amazing! Nothing can be more fulfilling and exciting than being part of such a process, where individuals, culture, and spiritual and political structures in the area are slowly being influenced by God and His people.

4. What's the best innovation you've helped create or extend?

When I was the TYS, we created and launched a concept we called "An Army for a New Generation." It was an attempt to reintroduce soldiership and junior soldiership to our young people, with a special focus on redefining junior soldiership and creating a new junior soldiers covenant. We also created a model for building a cell group structure to help teenagers from dysfunctional corps or corps without officers to take on responsibility for their own spiritual growth and find ways to reach out to their friends.

A few years ago, we felt that God was telling us to start a training school. The Christian church is losing ground in Europe, and yet most mission is focused on other continents. Once upon a time, when Europe was first evangelized, Gotland was a base for the Christian mission to the nations in the north of Europe. We believe that God again wants to use this island as a base for mission. So we sensed God's call to us to train missionaries, especially for Europe.

We therefore developed the Saved2Save Training School, a five-month training course for frontline soldiers based on Jesus' command: "Freely you have received, freely give." (Matthew 10:8) The first part of the course is focused on "saved," the experience of full salvation; the second part is focused on "2 save," communicating this salvation to others. The school is based at our local corps in Visby, Gotland.

The student body at S2S is truly international, with students coming from countries throughout Europe and from Africa and Australia as well. We hope for S2S to be a helpful tool in God's hand to re-evangelize this part of the world.

5. What's the best means of influence and how have you used it?

Nothing compares to personal one-to-one contact. We must of course use all available methods of communication to spread the Gospel and influence the world with Kingdom values. But as far as I have seen, God first of all works through people, in real-life relationships.

I believe in living together, fighting side by side, teaching by example, sharing success and failure. In short: the Jesus method of discipling. Obviously His method was God's method, and I believe it still is.

When I think about people I have influenced, I realize that I can see lasting fruit in the ones in whom I have invested time. It is individuals who build society, so there are no shortcuts in influencing society or the world. It is one individual to the other, person to person.

This is what we are trying to do through the Saved2Save Training School: give to others what God has given to us, multiply ourselves and what God has taught us over the years.

MAJOR KJELL KARLSTEN of the Sweden and Latvia Territory met Jesus Christ at the age of 15 at his home corps, Stockholm Vasa, and was enrolled as a soldier three years later (his family's fourth generation in the Army). He has served in corps and youth appointments throughout his officership. Before becoming an officer, Major Karlsten worked as an employed youth leader at his home corps. He married Ann-Christine in 1982, and they have three children. They started the Saved2Save training school in 2007. He still serves in Visby, on the island of Gotland, but also spends most of his time as territorial consultant for corps planting and pioneering, with Football for All (FFA) as the main catalyst. FFA, developed in Canada, uses soccer as a tool to reach at-risk youth. (www.ffaglobal. org)

WINNING THE WORLD FOR JESUS
MAJOR DANIELLE STRICKLAND

1. What is the best thing about being a Salvation Army officer?

The way it frees me to be about Kingdom business. Every facet of officership is about availability to God. My *job* is to listen and obey the Holy Spirit and to tell/demonstrate to everyone I can the love of Jesus.

It's an incredible opportunity to serve in that kind of capacity. I don't have to worry about paying the bills or making decisions based on financial or social pressures. I'm completely liberated to keep my eyes on the prize of God's Kingdom come.

Another amazing thing about officership is the fellowship of the fight. I'm connected to global leaders in a covenant of love. This covenant manifests itself in every selfless act for God's Kingdom all around the world through officers in more than 125 countries. Culture, language, economics, and geography separate us, yet we are bonded together in love through a covenant we share with God. This is a very deep and rich way to do life—in a global community of covenanted warriors. Together we win the world for Jesus!

2. What keeps you in officership when things are tough?

I remind myself of our history. There are great-hearts I've read about. I usually get out an old classic Army biography or a Catherine Booth book and re-read the primitive spirit and zeal of our early comrades and it spurs me on again. There are other great-hearts I've had the privilege of knowing. Sometimes I contact them, or I remember the encounters I've had and the encouragement and instruction they've given me over the years.

I try to do what David did and count the blessings of God. I remember the people that God has sent my way both to challenge and to change me, the faces and names of people whose lives have been transformed because we obeyed God together. This spurs me on.

I remember to fix my eyes on Jesus. Most times discouragement comes from focusing on earthly problems or issues. I try to lift my gaze. I look up. When I fix my eyes on Jesus, the long goal becomes visible, and I press on.

3. What is the greatest move of God you have experienced in an appointment?

Wow! I've had the privilege, many times, of God's great presence. I've had words of God spoken with power that have grown fruit in my own life. I've witnessed conversions that have transformed people from the inside out. I've been able to see healings and deliverance. I've had mentors and friends who have experienced instant miraculous answers to prayer. I've witnessed young people lose themselves in worship and in complete abandon through the Holy Spirit, with open confession and spontaneous conversions and holiness encounters. I'm not sure there is a "greatest," because all of them have been a tremendous privilege to be part of.

Sometimes the most extraordinary thing to me is the people who, despite great adversity, press on with God in willing and joyful obedience. This is an amazing thing to see.

4. What's the best innovation you've helped create or extend?

I think I mostly extend! Listening prayer has got to be up there. I've used Brad Jersak's tools in a book he wrote called *Can You Hear Me?* It's really about connecting people to hear the Spirit of Jesus for themselves. This has been an amazing journey for me, and to witness others develop their own dynamic, growing relationship with Jesus.

I've been part of developing some training in incarnational community in economically challenged neighborhoods. This has proven to be an effective mission extender.

Recently, I've been able to spur people on towards justice—which Cornel West defines as "love in public." Stop the Traffik is a global coalition that is thoroughly practical and useful for disseminating people's efforts and for mobilization.

5. What's the best means of influence and how have you used it?

Relationship is by far the best means of influence. The most fruit is born from relationship. In one sense, it seems the only Kingdom way—and yet God also uses our gifts.

I get to do a lot of speaking to big crowds. It sometimes feels like this is ineffective, because when I journey with people through relationship, I sense the richness of the experience and the fruit it bears. But I've been thrilled with the feedback I've received from my speaking. It seems that as I'm obedient to God in the gifts He gives me, He is faithful to grow and nurture the fruit.

So I'd say that my best means of influence is relationships, particularly in neighborhoods where I live. But beyond that, any obedient use of my gifts and skills, offered up with joy, has been effective for Kingdom growth.

MAJOR DANIELLE STRICKLAND of the Canada & Bermuda Territory has preached in 20 countries, written half a dozen books, earned a master's degree, and completed several triathlons and marathons. She has sparked such initiatives as The War College in Vancouver, B.C., several incarnational communities, and JUSTSalvos (Social Justice Salvation Army Australia). She is currently corps officer at Crossroads in Edmonton, Alberta.

NO CONFLICT, NO COMPROMISE

COMMISSIONER RAYMOND FINGER

1. What is the best thing about being a Salvation Army officer?

It is first of all being reconciled to the will of God. There is no conflict; there is no compromise. I am totally and absolutely content in the will of God. I am not inwardly fighting competing interests or agendas, not sitting in my seat during worship squirming over not being willing to release myself to what I know I have been called to by God.

Secondly, I get to be involved in the transformation of lives. I get to become part of the deep inward journey of other people. My officership gives me a sacred place that is trusted by others to the point where they are prepared to invite me into their very private and often uncertain worlds.

2. What keeps you in officership when things are tough?

What keeps any of us at what we are doing when things get tough? It is the powerful resolve to stay in it, unless for some compelling reason we cannot. I am completely resolved that there is nothing else that I want to do with my life than to be an officer and to serve God through this vocation. It was to this end that I was born and it will be to this purpose that I shall die.

There have been times when I have had my back up against the wall. There have been times when I have felt used and abused by people. There have been times when I have felt unappreciated, burnt out and burnt up. But here's the truth: God has always provided, and I just keep telling myself that there is no reason why He won't do it again.

My testimony is that God has never left me hanging out there bereft and He never will. He has always made a way. He has always restored me, and as a result I have been able to stand strong and get going again. It is amazing how long we can hold on by our fingernails when the floorboards have dropped out beneath our feet, because God always shows up and God always delivers. When it all seems hopeless, in some unexplained way the seas part and there is a way through it.

Here is the Bible text that lives in my brain at such moments, taken from the Phillips translation: "We are [hard pressed] on all sides, but we are never frustrated; we are puzzled, but never in despair. We are persecuted, but we never have to stand it alone: we may be knocked down but we are never knocked out!" (2 Corinthians 4:8–9)

3. What is the greatest move of God you have experienced in an appointment?

There is no end to the stories that can be told about the way in which God has moved in our midst. One of them is about our visit to the Democratic Republic of the Congo Kinshasa in October 2009.

The occasion was the 75th Anniversary Congress, five full days of meetings. More than 5,000 people gathered for the final Sunday afternoon meeting, which took place in the open with the temperature in the shade just over 40 degrees C (104 degrees F). The meeting had gone on for over four hours when I stood to give the final address, after which literally hundreds of people came forward for prayer, salvation, and restoration.

Many in pristine white uniforms came and knelt in the hot red dust, pouring out their hearts to God with loud cries and gestures of longing. With the sun beating down on them and perspiration running down their faces, nothing could distract them from their encounter with God as they knelt for an hour or more on the hard ground.

The spiritual fervor, passion, and energy were overwhelming. The atmosphere was palpitating as I became profoundly aware that no one other than God was in charge of that meeting, and there was nothing anyone could do other than stand back and watch the salvation of God unfold before our eyes.

I watched and I cried. Never before had I witnessed the presence of God manifest in such power and glory, in response to such simplicity and humility.

4. What's the best innovation you've helped create or extend?

We were serving a sizable, wealthy corps with many wonderful people meeting in a beautiful building. Our meetings were marked by magnificent expressions of music. It seemed to me that if people from the community wanted what The Salvation Army had to offer, they would have to go a long way to find a better example of Salvation Army worship. Yet no one was getting saved.

That being the case, God seemed to suggest that we needed to develop a parallel ministry that might resonate with the local community. Planning for a third Sunday meeting began. The concept was not without its challenges. The planning was meticulous; the corps council worked hard to ensure that it be rolled out in such a way as to be seen as a missional opportunity—but not everyone saw it that way.

After two years of prayer, planning, and publicity, the day finally arrived—and 110 people attended the first meeting. This soon settled into a regular gathering of 90 attendees. On its first-year anniversary, we celebrated the 33 people who had been saved, 15 who had become adherents, and three who had become senior soldiers.

5. What's the best means of influence and how have you used it?

It has to be people; it's always people. Surrounding yourself with people who are bigger and better, wiser and deeper than you are—that's influence.

It's also about watching people in their unguarded moments: who they are, what they say, how they say it, what they value, and how they live it. I love watching people: how they carry themselves, their gestures, and their posture and poise. I like to see how they wear clothes, how they treat their partners, and how they host others.

Lt. Colonel Pam Trigg once remarked that we are like a collage made up of the bits and pieces of other people we admire; we paste their best onto our lives to help make us the best we can be.

If you are looking for someone who can help you develop, do not restrict yourself to those around you; look for the best and go after them. I once asked a former premier of Western Australia for some guidance, thinking he would be much too busy to help me. To my surprise he agreed to meet me once a week at 7:30 a.m. for six consecutive weeks. The lesson being: Make "the ask" and leave it to them to decide if they are too busy to help.

COMMISSIONER RAYMOND FINGER of the Australia Southern Territory entered The Salvation Army Training College in 1971. During his active service, he led corps and served in courts, social youth services, the training college, candidates and leadership development, and on divisional staff. In 2006, he returned to Victoria, where he became territorial secretary for personnel. In 2007 he assumed the role of chief secretary. And in July 2010, the General appointed him territorial commander of his home territory. He and his wife, Commissioner Aylene Finger, are now retired.

CARRY ON WHERE I AM

COMMISSIONER LALKIAMLOVA

1. What is the best thing about being a Salvation Army officer?

To me, it is being a servant of God in an international organization that stands for meeting both spiritual and physical needs, with a focus on holiness and the fight against evil. As an officer of that organization, I feel I am a part of successes or failures anywhere in the Army world. I give thanks and praise to God when fellow officers, soldiers, territories, or commands are successful in their mission and pray for them when they fail. I am very aware that I am part of an international Christian family and not just an individual working on my own.

It is also being respected both inside and outside the Army and being able to intercede for individuals or families in whatever way they need me to. I feel privileged to be able to counsel, to pray, and to speak the Word of God to congregations and individuals alike. The fact that people allow you into their lives is proof of the way they trust an officer of The Salvation Army, and this is what I value the most.

2. What keeps you in officership when things are tough?

My officer's covenant, which I signed at the Mercy Seat, and my commitment to the call that I received from God. I am sustained by the strong and clear knowledge that what I am doing in the Army is not just between me and my leaders but also, and more importantly, between me and God. This commitment has developed and increased in my faith journey and is the main drive that helps me keep going.

The call I received when I was 18 years old was very clear to me, especially when it was confirmed by a challenge from one of the district officers of The Salvation Army. This officer wrote in the *War Cry* about the door that God had opened to evangelize a particular tribe in Assam State. As I read the article, I felt strongly that God was calling me to serve Him by preaching the saving message of his Gospel.

When I went to see the district officer whose article had challenged me to enter into full-time ministry, I thought he would make we welcome, but he did not. Instead, he warned me of all the difficulties I would face in serving God under him. I was very discouraged and even angry. The main thing he said was that he would not be able to give me any financial help and I would not survive with the amount of money that I had in hand. The people he wanted me to minister to were the poorest of the poor, and no help could be expected from them. There were no community development projects available in those days either. All we knew was preaching the Gospel.

All that the district officer had warned me about was true. I had no financial help from him except INR 20 (one pound) for the whole year of 1968. I taught in a school I had opened for the children and preached the Gospel to the families. But I had to build a shed to live in. I had to cut sun grass—the kind people used to roof their houses—and sell it in the market to earn my living. I was without food many times. I helped the womenfolk by climbing tall wild tropical trees and shaking off the fruit so that we could use the seeds for food. I gave thanks to God when someone invited me to eat jackfruit and gave me the seeds to take home.

To add to all this, I received news that the entire village where I had left my mother and sister had been burned by the military, leaving every family with only the clothes they were standing up in. I then asked myself, *Should I leave my ministry and return home to help my mother and sister settle elsewhere?* I knew that if I did, no one would take care of the new Christians and the school I had started. The answer was "No." I felt that I should carry on where I was. My mother understood this very well and agreed to deal with her circumstances by herself.

These kinds of problems and difficulties persisted throughout the first three years of my officership. Malaria was our long-staying guest! The difficulty was due to the poverty of the people and the absence of any kind of medical or other help, even from the Army. The allowance we received was far from sufficient, and I confess that there were times when I felt I did not get the appreciation I felt I deserved. That shook the relationship between me and my leaders. In this situation the tempter knocked on my door very often.

In such moments of confusion, the Holy Spirit reminded me that my ministry covenant was not between me and my leaders but between me and my God, who will surely acknowledge my suffering with a smile and a crown in Heaven. His call for me to serve Him, my commitment to that call, and His clear and obvious presence with me keeps me in my officership to this day.

3. What is the greatest move of God you have experienced in an appointment?

After only four years of my officership, I was selected by our leaders for a very challenging appointment: to open a school for the blind in the state of Mizoram. The government of that state had made a request for The Salvation Army to open such a school. The government would provide land and a stipend for students. So it was that in 1975, after being stationed in a small corps of only about 15 families, I was sent to the Army's School for the Blind in the state of Kalimpong. There I would learn Braille and observe the system of administration under Brigadier Dorothy Page, an officer from Canada.

I was asked to try to learn to read Braille with my fingers. As I could not make out even a single letter, I thought I was being asked to do an impossible task, one I would never be able to master—let alone to open a new school. But instead of giving up, I asked my tutor to allow me to try with my eyes. She agreed and I then made considerable improvement; within six months I learned English Braille and was able to help transcribe textbooks for the students at the school.

However, the main challenge facing me was to form Braille script in my own language, which was very significant if I was to start a new school in my home state. In the following year, as I continued to strive, I became more confident and was gradually able to form Braille script in my own language. I felt as if I were bringing down the walls of Jericho and I praised God for my success in completing the task He had given me. In 1976 I transcribed all the primary level textbooks into the newly created Mizo Braille. We were able to return with them at the beginning of 1977 to start the new school at Kolasib, Mizoram.

In the beginning, only a few families wanted to send their blind children. Others did not want to for two reasons: One is that they didn't believe that a blind child could ever learn in a school; until that time Braille script was not known to the people of Mizoram, and no one ever thought that blind people could go to school to learn and live an independent life. The second was because they did not want to add more burdens to their blind child, who had already had enough suffering in his or her life.

To change such a notion about blindness was going to be a big challenge for me. A few months after the opening, I took the few students we had and conducted public meetings in most of the big towns in the state. Our students showed what they could do, such as reading the alphabet and telling the time from a Braille wristwatch. It worked well, and later two more schools were opened in the state by another organization. Many blind students have graduated. More than 10 of my students are now working in the government with handsome salaries and have become not only independent, but also able to support their families. The Bible in Mizo Braille was printed and I was called on to oversee the proofreading.

4. What is the best innovation you have helped create or extend?

The System of Self-Support in India Eastern Territory is one of the best innovations that I helped in my officership. In 1985, my wife and I were appointed as leaders of the Central Division, the largest division in India East. The headquarters are in Aizawl, the capital of the state of Mizoram, where there are about 60 corps. When we were appointed to the division, only five corps were able to provide a full allowance for their corps officers. The rest could only give half and even one-quarter; the remaining money had to be received from the International Self-Denial Fund. Along with the staff, I took on the challenge of helping the soldiers with tithing to enable the whole division to become fully self-supporting. We discussed and taught the subject of tithing with the local officers in every corps and stressed the importance of self-support. Our slogans were "Giving is worship" and "To be self-supporting is to be mature."

In 1986, the divisional budget session was convened at one of the corps halls. Present were all the officers of the division, three local officers from each corps, and two from each society (a group who meets as The Salvation Army but are smaller than a corps or outpost). I presented the faith budget for 1986–87 that I had prepared. The idea of involvement of soldiers in discussion of the budget was well accepted. Every member was actively involved in the discussion, which lasted from morning to evening. In the evening, the budget was accepted with just a few amendments. The follow-up from the corps and societies was excellent, as the decision had been made by representatives of every corps.

In 1988, I was appointed as territorial self-support and evangelism secretary. In that appointment, I visited all the divisions of the territory. (The territory later was divided into two territories, India North and India East.) I introduced the concept of involving soldiers to motivate them in their tithing and giving and in the self-support program. I helped every division to make it their policy to present the budget to the local officers. The other six divisions in the present India East Territory—apart from Central—became self-supporting that year.

Two decades later, the system continued to grow, with every corps and society in the territory giving 60 percent of their income to territorial headquarters for self-support. Every officer of the territory receives his/her full allowance, and the financial position of the territory has become much stronger.

5. What is the best means of influence and how have you used it?

Being pragmatic, being an example without a murmur, is the secret of my influence, which I maintain under all circumstances. I accept whatever appointment or task is given to me by my leaders in the Army as coming from God. I know I am a soldier of God in the Army, and that demands total obedience to the leaders. I have mentioned a few of my sufferings. In all of my officership, I have never murmured or complained because of problems and difficulties.

From the beginning of my ministry, I have had a heart for outreach evangelism. I do that without counting the cost. During 1985-88, God gave me the chance to use my influence as a divisional leader. We reached out to new areas and convened missionary conventions where I challenged our soldiers for mission. After three years, about 60 people had dedicated their lives to be Soldiers of the Cross (missionaries); all were posted to remote non-Christian villages to evangelize. All of them were sponsored by individuals, corps, and departments of corps, without affecting corps contributions for divisional self-support.

God gave me a wider appointment as territorial evangelism secretary, and that opened the door for me to use my influence on more people. I was able to convene more missionary conventions. I traveled as far as Nepal, Sikkim in the Himalayas, and to the central part of India for evangelism. We were able to open fire in Sikkim, and that work continues to grow. The Spirit is so much alive, and the territory now has more 260 Soldiers of the Cross who are committed to the mission to save souls without counting the cost. Each of these was sponsored by an individual soldier, family, corps, Home League, or youth group.

Silent suffering for the cause influences people and brings forth fruit.

COMMISSIONER LALKIAMLOVA is an officer from the India Eastern Territory, which has its headquarters in the State of Mizoram. Prior to officership he worked as a Soldier of the Cross for three years. He entered the training college as a member of the Light Bringers session and was commissioned in 1971. He holds two degrees, a B.A. and a B.Div. He and his wife, Commissioner Lalhlimpuii, served as chief secretary and territorial secretary for women's ministries in the India South-West Territory and as territorial leaders in India Central. Their last appointments before retirement were as international secretary and zonal secretary for women's ministries for South Asia. They have three adult children and three lovely grandchildren.

GETTING THROUGH BY THE GRACE OF GOD

COMMISSIONER WESLEY HARRIS

1. What is the best thing about being a Salvation Army officer?

The sense of solidarity with comrades around the world and the reputation that often opens doors that might otherwise be closed. For a number of years I accompanied the Camberwell Corps Band for Sunday morning open-air meetings and visited from door to door. I made contact with many hundreds of people and *without one rebuff!* But for my uniform and what it represented, the response might have been very different. Many good people had contributed to the corporate image of the Army and prepared the way for me.

For a brief period following retirement I took charge of a small country corps. With my wife, I visited all on the soldiers roll in a couple of days and wondered what else I could do in a limited period. I decided that I would walk around the town in my uniform every day and greet everyone I met. Responses were varied, but none were negative, because my uniform spoke for me even before I opened my mouth. The commissioner was humbly proud to be greeted as the Army captain and reveled in the opportunity to have such a role full time.

2. What keeps you in officership when things are tough?

It would be ridiculous to suggest that there have not been tough times during my 60-plus years as an officer—not that officership has a monopoly on difficulties, for they can come in every walk of life. I was appointed to the famous Regent Hall Corps in the center of London at a time of unprecedented difficulty with much negative publicity. But by the grace of God we got through.

Personally, I have never for an instant thought of quitting officership since the pivotal moment when, at 17 years of age, I had a "God moment" and knew that I was called. But that temptation has come to better people than me. Others have different challenges. Some may abandon officership not so much because of overstrain, but because of "under-motive."

3. What is the greatest move of God you have experienced in an appointment?

A few days before I was to conduct Youth Councils in the Eastern Victoria Division, I learned that due to a double booking, a theatrical company had been given permission to take over the venue at 7:30 p.m. for what I believe was a rehearsal of *Guys and Dolls!* An additional piece of information was that the platform on which leaders would be seated was hydraulically controlled and might be lowered at the push of a button—and that at the time when I had planned to appeal for seekers!

On the day, I condensed proceedings as much as possible, but the Holy Spirit was not to be hurried. There was one of the largest movements to the Mercy Seat I had ever seen in Youth Councils, and as the clock ticked towards 7:30 p.m., I rejoiced—and yet feared that at any moment the platform might be lowered with me on it! I know of those who made meaningful commitments for officership or other service on that occasion when everything seemed to be going wrong, but God made everything come wonderfully right.

4. What's the best innovation you've helped create or extend?

I have long believed that unless we innovate we will enervate. But innovating can sometimes cause us to live dangerously! The only real failure may be a failure to try, but that may still be scary. Like others, I may have been the author of some monumental flops but here—putting modesty on the altar—I recall, to the glory of God, an innovation that has endured for over 40 years.

In 1964, my wife and I were appointed as corps officers to Croydon Citadel in the United Kingdom. A 2,000-seat concert hall had just been opened in the district and I felt we should hire it for a goodwill service of carols, when the collection would go to a well-known charity. Some criticized raising money for a non-Army cause and others—including the mayor—were sure we could never fill such a building. However, we worked very hard, and on the night had to turn hundreds away. Within a couple of years we had to have three sittings for the service with close on 6,000 in attendance; and 40 years later we went back to see that what had become a local tradition was still being maintained.

5. What's the best means of influence and how have you used it?

Means of influence must vary from person to person. Sometimes we will be unconscious of the way in which we have influenced others. The Holy Spirit may be using us most when we are least aware of what is happening.

Apart from my duties as an officer in corps and headquarters appointments, I have tried to let my pen do the talking through many hundreds of articles and various books. In retirement I belong to a writers group composed of some nonbelievers and others of various faiths. Members read what they have written, be it poetry or fiction or whatever, and then the item is discussed. I write a weekly article—sometimes of general interest but at other times an expression of my Christian faith—and I pray that by these means I may bear a good witness.

COMMISSIONER WESLEY HARRIS hails from the United Kingdom with the Republic of Ireland Territory. He was the first colonel nominated by the High Council for General, commanded three territories, and authored nine books. In retirement the commissioner taught religious education in Australian public schools for 15 years and has served on various international boards, including The War College and Go For Souls.

A TASTE OF HEAVEN ON EARTH

COLONEL JANET MUNN

1. What is the best thing about being a Salvation Army officer?

The potential for unencumbered focus on the mission of Jesus Christ to the world for whom He gave His life. Obviously there are also many pitfalls that can distract—but in my experience of officership, many structures are in place to liberate the officer for mission. That is how I have tried to live as an officer, and continue to: Just focus on what Jesus would have me be and do in whatever context I'm in. Simple. Not easy.

2. What keeps you in officership when things are tough?

My sense of commitment to the Lord and His leading me to The Salvation Army. I see His hand in the circumstances throughout my youth and young adult years that brought me to the Army. I've made a commitment to Him in becoming an officer and I want to be true to my commitments. Only once in 28 years of officership have I actually felt like quitting. I simply asked Jesus if I could leave, and He simply, gently answered, "No." That was quite a few years ago and I've never needed to ask Him again.

Also, it would be naïve to think that there is any place, or any group, or any ministry, that would be ideal for a life dedicated to Jesus. Every context has its strengths and weaknesses. The Salvation Army is my context.

And I love the mission of The Salvation Army, the sense of community, and the opportunities for women (though there's plenty of room for improvement in this).

3. What is the greatest move of God you have experienced in an appointment?

While I was stationed at THQ in USA East, the territory committed to a year of 24/7 prayer—June to June. This ignited at divisional summer camps across the territory. Every camp established a prayer room and committed to at least a week of 24/7. Some continued all summer—eight weeks. Not surprisingly, there was much significant spiritual breakthrough throughout that summer.

Also, the sense of unity across the territory was palpable. Many corps, rehab centers, and divisional headquarters set up 24/7 prayer rooms.

THQ in New York started the year of nonstop prayer by taking the first week of 24/7. The territorial leaders at the time dedicated space in the main meeting hall of THQ to be transformed into a large, active prayer room. Toward the end of that one-week commitment, the need to continue was obvious, so THQ had a nonstop prayer room for weeks, and that space was utilized for prayer for several months. Miracles were happening in the prayer room, in the boardrooms, and in peoples' lives throughout that time.

4. What's the best innovation you've helped create or extend?

Spearheading the year of 24/7 prayer was a valuable and blessed opportunity for me. I believe it made a lasting spiritual impact in many lives and on many places. We tasted Heaven on Earth for a season, which whetted our appetite for more.

Initiating a culture of small-group accountability for officers is something I've invested in deeply over the years. This has been of great benefit to many officers in terms of their spiritual well-being, emotional health, morale, and perseverance in ministry.

I've also been committed to a lifestyle of prayer and fasting as the first work of the Christian, even as Jesus withdrew to the wilderness for 40 days of prayer and fasting as His first work prior to His public ministry. This is countercultural with respect to the affluent societies in which I've lived, but it is the way of Christ.

In USA East, I was part of the pioneering years of the arts ministry, which has now flourished, with thousands of young people participating in arts programs within The Salvation Army. Many have gone on to study the arts in higher education, and many have found a place of belonging, of worship, of identity in Christ as a result.

5. What's the best means of influence and how have you used it?

To be as wholehearted for Christ as I can be, and to never give up. This is my desire and my intention, and thus I influence people all around me. It's amazing to see what the Lord does through my weak but sincere efforts, life, and witness.

COLONEL JANET MUNN of the USA Eastern Territory, who holds a D.Min. in transformational leadership from Ashland Theological Seminary, served most recently as the training principal at the School for Officer Training in Sydney, Australia, and has been appointed training principal at the College for Officer Training in USA East. She gave many years of her life to summer camping ministries for underprivileged children and youth. In contexts ranging from local to regional to international, she has called people to 24/7 prayer, corporate fasting, and accountability and discipleship. She is passionate about the fullness of Christ being manifest in this generation. Colonel Munn is the daughter of a Nazarene pastor–father and a disciple–making mother, the wife of an Anglo–American egalitarian husband, and the mother of two beautiful, articulate, and blessed young adults.

NOT A CONTRACT, BUT A COMMITMENT
LT. COLONEL CHECK YEE

1. What is the best thing about being a Salvation Army officer?

- Living practically in a born-again life.
- Appreciating the full trust that comes with ordination for service by the Army.
- Upholding the Army's heritage in joyful, spirited worship.
- Being part of the warm international fellowship of the Army.
- Having basic needs provided for in a moderate living style.
- Serving not under a contract of human employment but within a commitment unto God.
- Seeing people's lives change for the better as they find hope, learn that they are loved, and learn to love.
- Having authority to approach the masses as an ambassador of the Gospel and save the perishing.
- Wearing the uniform proudly as a testimony of Christian faith and mission.

2. What keeps you in officership when things are rough?

Some rough things I have experienced:

- An over-enthusiastic advisory board member holding a

committee meeting and ignoring my participation.
- A local officer charging me falsely and teaming up with others against me.
- Public misunderstanding of the Army's mission.
- A barren Mercy Seat.
- A letter of complaint against me sent to DHQ.

What keeps me going is that I take all my anxiety to God.

I have counseled countless multitudes throughout my years of service. I prayed with them and instructed them to do likewise. When I have my own challenges, why can't I also do the same?

My lesson learned is that no vocation or mission is without problems as long as people are involved. It is part of being alive.

I must be true to my vows made on the day of my commissioning. As the chorus goes: "No turning back, no turning back."

3. What is the greatest move of God you have experienced in an appointment?

I had only one appointment in all my 35 years of active service as a Salvation Army officer. The Holy Spirit convinced me not to think the grass was greener on the other side of the fence. "You come to serve," He said, "anywhere and any time."

For 35 years in the same corps, I never ran out of inspiration as to what to preach on Sunday, nor did I repeat an old sermon. The best one I preached is the one I preached this morning. I have never considered myself an eloquent or powerful orator, but I take delight in sharing what God wants me to say in an honest way with people who come from far and near to hear His Word.

4. What's the best innovation you've created or extended?

In 1962, when someone complained out loud, "This is America, speak English!" I started preaching both in Chinese and English in our meetings.

When I remembered how I was attracted to the Army by its marching bands and open-air meetings, I organized a March of Witness, which has become an annual community event for the past 29 years.

When I marveled at the instant playback of the video camera in 1977, I began my own television program, "The High Places," 30 minutes of music, testimony, and devotional talk with the theme, "To discover the extraordinary in an ordinary day." I learned how to write, direct, host, and produce from an old book in a junk pile entitled "How to Produce a Television Program" that I purchased for $1. This bilingual program lasted for 18 fruitful years and reached out to thousands in the community. Some attended the corps and enrolled as soldiers. I believe it was the only such corps-based program in the Army world.

When I realized the power of the press, I began contributing religious articles to two local newspapers on a weekly basis and continued regularly for more than 20 years. One of the eight books I wrote, *Banners Unfurled*, won the Literary Award of the Taiwan Chinese Overseas Commission in 1979.

I write letters of comfort to needy individuals reported in the news or letters of encouragement to people I have never met. Some consequently become friends.

Forgive my "bragging." Believe me, I am simply counting God's blessings. My true desire is that all honor and glory goes to Him who sent me.

5. What's the best means of influence and how have you used it?

I am tremendously challenged by our pioneer officers, how they faced persecution and hardship courageously. They are my heroes in the faith. I must do no less to be worthy of being their descendant.

My eyes have also witnessed many officers of the present time whose integrity, compassion, and sacrifice have inspired me to be humble and always alert to "Do something."

LT. COLONEL CHECK YEE, O.F., was born in China and survived Japan's invasion of his homeland during World War II. As a journalist, he fled from the Communist regime just before the country dropped the Bamboo Curtain and became isolated from the rest of the world for the next 30 years.

For all 35 years of his active service with his wife, Lt. Colonel Phyllis Mah, Yee led the San Francisco Chinatown Corps in his home territory, USA West. He traveled widely and authored eight books, including *Good Morning China*. His Sunday night television program gave him the opportunity to share the Gospel and mobilize funds for mercy missions. In 1987, General Eva Burrows presented him with the Certificate of Exceptional Service. In 1997, in retirement, he was admitted to the Order of the Founder, the Army's highest honor, by General Paul Rader.

COMPELLED TO RESPOND

COMMISSIONER GARTH McKENZIE

1. What is the best thing about being a Salvation Army officer?

After leaving high school, I was employed in a large department store, undertaking a management-training program. This included part-time university and New Zealand Institute of Management study. I received rapid promotion, being responsible for the introduction of decimal currency training for over 200 staff, then personnel manager, and, two years later, manager of a newly opened branch store.

I had attended Wellington City Corps from Sunday School days. I was young people's sergeant-major and youth group leader for four years as well as in the senior band. Each year the Wellington City band was the duty band for commissioning. Over the years, I was constantly challenged by the cadets and their testimonies as they were commissioned.

I was due to receive my 10-year service pen from the managing director of my company, with the expectation of a gold watch after 30 years of service. However, the Spirit of God compelled me to respond to the invitation on a Sunday evening of commissioning as I sensed a clear word in my mind to be an officer. Mel, my wife, had also experienced a clear call to officership but didn't want to respond unless I made the decision first. I gave 13 months' notice and we entered training college with our baby daughter in 1973.

The best thing about being a Salvation Army officer ... peace with God, freedom of being in His will, fulfillment, making a difference in people's lives. Receiving many, many letters as our retirement approached from officers, soldiers, and people I worked with at the territorial level indicating that their lives have been helped, changed for good and for God, due to my influence.

2. What keeps you in officership when things are tough?

God's call, my covenant, personal commitment, people's trust in me, wise counsel from my wife and Christian friends. Recognition of Satan's strategies.

Example: While I was in senior leadership, a number of allegations of child abuse emerged from people who had been in Salvation Army children's homes during the 1960s and early '70s. Other churches were also being faced with these allegations. Similar allegations in Australia seemed to have triggered this in New Zealand. Regretfully, some of these allegations—the majority—were found to be true, although some were false. Handling this matter was tough.

3. What is the greatest move of God you have experienced in an appointment?

After prayerful consultation, my first major initiative on becoming TC was a territory-wide call to 24/7 prayer for a full year commencing in March 2005. Such was the response that 24/7 was extended for another year. After that, many corps continued to hold 24/1,2,3,4,5,6,7 prayer at various times.

Direct outcomes from this initiative included the Territorial Strategic Mission Plan (TSMP) 2006/2010, the second chapter of which was to be introduced with six months of 24/7 prayer culminating in a territorial congress; New Zeal, a Roots/Aggressive Christianity-type territorial event; answered prayer; healing; and fresh personal renewal. Full coverage of the 24/7 initiative is given in Major Judith Bennett's book *White Cloud Soaring*.

4. What's the best innovation you've helped create or extend?

The Territorial Strategic Mission Plan 2006/2010. Goals:

- To grow all Salvationists as dynamic disciples.
- To increase the number of new soldiers.
- To take significant steps towards the eradication of poverty in New Zealand, Fiji, and Tonga.
- To be a connected, streamlined, mission-focused Army.

We retained the territory's vision statement that had been in place for many years: To help people, transform lives, reform society through God in Christ by the Holy Spirit's power.

There have been many positive outcomes from the TSMP:

- The launch, with 98 percent of all active officers attending along with center managers and invited local officers—an outstanding event.
- DELVE—a new version of future officers weekends—linked with 24/7 prayer, resulted in the largest number of cadets in 20 years.
- New emphasis on soldier-making and discipling.
- Positive action on the other goals, including outstanding "Just Action" social conferences.

5. What's the best means of influence and how have you used it?

Stressed spiritual growth, prayer, and Bible reading. Demonstrated integrity in all dealings even when it would have easy to give only some of the story.

As TC I was sometimes involved in protracted negotiations on major property deals. One being settled late on a Friday evening in my office involved the head of a family trust and her legal advisors. I had a group of senior officers with me. The legal advisors, after the price had been settled, insisted on a written undertaking then and there. Due to a number of factors, we were not able to do this until Monday morning. I gave my word we would follow through on Monday. Against her legal advisors, the head of the family trust said, "The commissioner has given his word. That's God's word to me." Very humbling.

COMMISSIONER GARTH McKENZIE, from the New Zealand, Fiji, and Tonga Territory, retired in 2009 after 34 years of active officership. Appointments included corps ministry; special efforts; youth, divisional, and territorial leadership; and five years as a territorial forces military chaplain serving with infantry and medical units. Prior to serving in exchange appointments in the Australia Southern Territory, he and his wife, Mel, were divisional leaders in the Northern Division and in Perth, Western Australia. They were appointed to Territorial Headquarters Melbourne, where he was secretary for personnel. On his return to New Zealand in 2002, he was appointed chief secretary and in June 2004, became territorial commander. In retirement Garth spends three days a week at Booth College of Mission as mission training officer.

IN TEARS AT THE MERCY SEAT

MAJOR ST DULA

1. What is the best thing about being a Salvation Army officer?

The best thing about being an officer and wearing the uniform is the opportunity it gives to serve others through the love of Christ.

2. What keeps you in officership when things are tough?

First, I signed a covenant of officership, with tears, at the Mercy Seat.

Second, my mother, a member of the Presbyterian Church, wears her silver star everywhere. She is proud that her son is a servant of the Most High, a Salvation Army officer.

3. What is the greatest move of God you have experienced in an appointment?

By God's grace, we served as corps officers for over 10 years. The TC sent me to bring peace and reconciliation to a corps that had split. Many members had left the Army. Though my health was very weak, I fasted many days and nights. I spent most of my time at the Mercy Seat in tears praying over the roll book of the corps. I carried the Army flag in the street, visiting the houses of Salvationists and non-

Salvationists and kneeling down in their sitting rooms with the flag. After many months, a great revival broke out in the corps. We conducted a self-denial campaign in every night meeting for six months. Praise the Lord. God moved with signs and wonders.

While serving as territorial evangelist and secretary, I traveled extensively. God was with us, and we saw the great hand of God raising the dead, removing brain tumors, banishing cancer, and many other signs and wonders under the blood of Jesus Christ at the Mercy Seat.

4. What's the best innovation you've helped create or extend?

Like William Booth and Frederick Booth-Tucker, I am a servant with a passion for lost souls.

5. What's the best means of influence and how have you used it?

Prayer life, servant leadership, charismatic teaching, and disciplinary leadership.

MAJOR SANGTHANGDULA (ST DULA) of the India Eastern Territory met Christ in 1981. Before his conversion, he says, he was like gang leader Nicky Cruz of the United States. He attended college but left to enter the Salvation Army Training College with his wife, C. Malsawmi, in 1984. In 24 years of active ministry, they served as corps officers, in training work, at THQ, in outreach, as territorial evangelists, in finance, and as divisional leaders.

ST Dula holds four doctorates (missiology, Christian counseling, evangelism, and an honorary D.D.). An effective evangelist and revivalist, he has held many important posts in the ecumenical movement. He is founder and president of Mizoram Media Evangelical Ministries (IT) and Telephone Counseling Ministries of Mizoram. He and his wife are now retired.

A CATALYST FOR CHANGE

MAJOR SHAR DAVIS

1. What is the best thing about being a Salvation Army officer?

I get to share in people's journey with God and sometimes be the catalyst for change as they get a revelation of who they are in Christ and what He is calling them to be. I love to see people's potential realized and see them walking in the fullness of their identity and destiny. It is about calling people to something greater than what they see in themselves, making prophetic declarations over people and partnering with them as they allow the Holy Spirit to do His transforming work in their lives.

Example: I invited a couple who had never spoken to me about officership to attend DELVE, our officership exploration weekend. After getting over the initial shock at my invitation, they went. God did an amazing work in their lives over the next few months, and the couple were sent to training.

2. What keeps you in officership when things get tough?

First, and most importantly, my absolute belief that God has called me to be a Salvation Army officer and that that call was made knowing full well both my strengths and my weaknesses. When God called me He knew what I would have the capacity for, and I strongly believe that God will equip me for anything He calls me to do. This call is strengthened by my sense of destiny—what God has called me to do within the Salvation Army.

Secondly, I stay because I wholeheartedly believe in The Salvation Army and its position and purpose within our world. I believe God has not finished with The Salvation Army and that our best days are ahead of us. I do not want to miss out on making history as we advance the Kingdom of God, as Heaven invades Earth, and as we see lives transformed from darkness to light, from brokenness to wholeness, from death to life.

Example: I was told I was moving and given the location of my new appointment. I was extremely excited, particularly as I had friends and a very special goddaughter there. I began to dream and vision for this new appointment.

One week before farewell orders were to be announced, I was rung and told the appointment had changed. My new appointment was one place I had told God I never wanted to be appointed to (silly, I know). Everything within me was devastated, and I could not understand the logic of the change. I was asked to simply accept the change and go. I replied that I would keep my word of never refusing an appointment, but that it would take some time for my heart to accept this change. I believe God really honored my willingness to go, as it was just a short time after the move when I felt such a sense of belonging and purpose to the appointment.

3. What is the greatest move of God you have experienced in an appointment?

For me, it is always what God is up to in the here and now. Each time God moves in someone's life is a miracle. Each answered prayer and every time the reality of Heaven invades the reality of Earth is the greatest moment!

At Grandview Corps, God moved in awesome ways. We found ourselves in the midst of a wave of huge stretching and amazement as we recognized what God was up to. We saw Him provide fantastic financial resources for individuals and the corps as a whole as we prayed. We saw relationships restored between fathers and daughters, between husbands and wives, between siblings. God instantly set a man free of a 20-year-plus addiction to pornography, tobacco, and alcohol; healed a woman of back pain she had suffered for over 20 years; and healed a baby of a hole in its heart. And God brought a dead man back to life. The guy died again later on (Editor's note: so did Lazarus!), but he came back to life all the same.

For weeks I had been saying that if Jesus could raise people from the dead, and the same Holy Spirit who empowered Him empowers us, surely we too can raise people from the dead. One Sunday I said to the corps, "I believe it. I just have never come across a dead person I could pray for." The next Saturday our corps was having a working bee on a street corner, when a man riding a scooter across the intersection had a heart attack and died. A corps member and I raced to him and moved him onto the road. A cardiac nurse arrived on scene and started chest compressions. The corps lady started pumping the bag and I thought, What shall I do? I heard the Spirit say, "You asked for a dead man. Well, what are you going to do?"

So I grabbed the man's hand and started praying that somehow he would know Jesus, that it wouldn't be too late for him, and that the Holy Spirit would breathe His breath into him and give him life again. To make a long story short, we found that he was coming to. He squeezed my hand and took a breath and his pulse started up again.

The corps lady and I both exclaimed, "He's breathing!" The nurse said, "IMPOSSIBLE!" I heard the Holy Spirit say to me, "Who will you choose to believe—a nurse? Or will you believe that the very thing you have just prayed for has happened, that I have breathed life into this man?" I chose the Holy Spirit over the nurse.

The man was taken to hospital and died later on that day. I realize it's not as cool as if he was walking around testifying to being brought back from the dead. But I'm OK with the fact that God is teaching me to bring Heaven to Earth in the midst of all circumstances and despite the circumstances. I'm still believing and praying for the day when I personally see the dead rise and testify to the saving power of God.

4. What's the best innovation you have helped create or extend?

In Dunedin, I established a flat next to the corps for Christians who were interested in incarnational ministry to the people in our community. It became an open home, a focal point for university students and others, with people coming for meals or just dropping in to talk. We would often have 15 people crammed into our lounge room eating roast and apple crumble and talking about matters of faith and life and the connection between the two. I was moved at the end of that year, but since then the flat has continued and become even more intentional and a second flat was established in another house in the area. These houses are an important part of the presence of the corps within the community.

We had 40 independent living units connected to the Grandview Corps. Rather than see them simply as a financial interest for the corps, I employed a "pastoral carer," who was responsible for the pastoral/spiritual care of the villagers. We ran a Bible study and prayer meeting in the village each week. Many of the villagers participated in corps events, some began attending meetings, and a few went through soldiership preparation classes. We were also able to provide villagers with addiction services and community ministries. We continued to look for ways to connect these people to the mission and ministry of the corps. We set up a prayer support system for corps people to "adopt" a unit and be responsible for bringing that household before the Lord in prayer.

5. What's the best means of influence and how have you used it?

To demonstrate the Kingdom of Heaven and the power of God in my own life as I live in relationship with others. I cannot give something to others that I do not have, and people will catch what I have, not what I say. I try and live as transparently as possible. I recognize that my personal journey towards wholeness in God is a tool that He uses to unlock truths for other people. My willingness to be vulnerable before others and not hide behind the uniform or position has opened doors of ministry. As I demonstrate the goodness of God, people are drawn towards Him to experience that goodness for themselves.

I am influenced most by those who invest themselves into my life. Those who are already walking in areas of faith and Kingdom life that I desire to walk in are some of the most attractive people around. Why waste time with those who are no better off than we are? If we want to kill giants we need to hang out with giant-killers. The very best life I can live is one that requires God to turn up—and if He doesn't, I'm sunk!

MAJOR SHAR DAVIS of the New Zealand, Fiji, and Tonga Territory, turned up, under duress, at The Salvation Army when she was 10 years old and has never left! She has held positions in divisional youth and children's ministries, has been in sole charge of corps, has been part of a team ministry corps (merging three corps into one), and currently serves at Aranui Corps and ministers in the streets of Christchurch. Her studies are toward a double degree—a B.A. in Maori studies and a B.Th. She is passionate about the Kingdom of God and seeing Heaven invade Earth.

SECURITY IN MY LIFE'S PURPOSE
MAJOR DOUG HAMMOND

1. What is the best thing about being a Salvation Army officer?

Well, if I had the time and patience, I'm certain that I could write a book on this question. However, I don't think anyone would find it interesting. I'm not being modest when I say that. I really feel that my relationship with God, my calling, etc., are so personal that what I would write, although very exciting to me, would be dull for others.

The best part of officership for me is a security in my life's purpose. I have a true sense of peace in my life that I'm in the place where I was created to be.

2. What keeps you in officership when things are tough?

I don't think about leaving. Not seriously anyway.

Example? We didn't have a great Sunday yesterday, but I did not think about quitting.

Sorry to be so simplistic, but I really think that's all it is. When I do have a tough time, I take opportunities to get away, try and get my mind off hassles for a while—pray, read, exercise, watch a movie, go to a game, etc. I suspect that when we get too consumed with hassles we become fatigued, and our minds start to wander in places where they should not be.

3. What is the greatest move of God you have experienced in an appointment?

Too many. But oftentimes I've almost missed God's working because I'm preoccupied with my stuff.

For three years my wife and I worked in Benoni, South Africa, with a corps and a goodwill center that included a shelter for homeless families. The last month before we left was particularly discouraging. A number of families fell apart, some recovering addicts relapsed, a person we trusted stole some money and took off, etc. It was a tough month as we were preparing to go.

On our journey to our next appointment, we decided to take a mini-vacation at a motel that had a pool. We spent a day playing with the kids and hanging out at the pool. This small, cheap motel in the middle of nowhere was perfect for what we needed. The place was almost deserted. There was just one girl playing in the pool other than our kids, and her mother sat on the side watching her. Karen and I sat talking over the events of the previous month—somewhat shell-shocked. As we spoke, it began to feel like our last three years had been a total waste of time. Even though the sun was shining, it was turning into a dark moment for us.

As we sat there recounting one disaster after another, the woman sitting by the side of the pool—the only other adult in sight—got up and walked over to us. "Are you Lieutenant Hammond? Do you remember me? I'm … " The woman had stayed at our shelter with her family two years earlier. Karen remembered her slightly; I had no idea who she was. She said she and her husband had gone through a difficult time and ended up at the Salvation Army goodwill shelter. The shelter had been a great encouragement to them. They got jobs, got on their feet, got a place to live. It was a nice story she shared with us. The timing was perfect.

Was that the biggest move of God in our ministry? I don't know. I do know that it reminded me that God can supply our needs in ways we never imagine. Just as we were sinking into despair, God had us cross paths with a woman who was a huge encouragement to us. Suddenly we were reminded of dozens of success stories. Suddenly the sun seemed to be really shining.

4. What's the best innovation you've helped create or extend?

The goodwill center in South Africa was a concept I walked into, but it was blessed in a special way while we were there. We housed and fed 90 people, ran a low-cost day care for domestic workers, and fed up to 100 street people a day. We were very strategic about presenting the Gospel in all areas of our services. The coolest thing was that while we were there we developed a model that helped the center to be self-sufficient financially. We had no government, DHQ, THQ, or overseas finance. It was completely supported from the community.

I was also very encouraged by the ministry we developed at Mountain View Hospital. Mountain View was an AIDS hospital where someone died every day. While we were there the necessity of the Gospel became so clear to us. It was our policy that nobody was allowed to die without hearing the Gospel—in Zulu—and having opportunity to respond. I wonder how many people I will run into in Heaven as a result of our time at Mountain View.

5. What's the best means of influence and how have you used it?

First of all, I'd suggest relationship. No substitute.

Second, I would offer service. When people see you in a servant role they are somewhat disarmed in terms of seeing you as anything negative.

Third, I suspect we have drastically underestimated the power of Bible-based preaching.

MAJOR DOUG HAMMOND and his wife, Major Karen Hammond, of the Canada & Bermuda Territory, have served in Uganda, South Africa, and Canada, where they are currently corps officers in a multi-ethnic setting at Bloor Central Corps in Toronto. Doug runs long distances and plays rugby. Having trained with the Navigators, he enjoys being a discipler.

A CONSTANT LIFE OF BATTLE

LIEUTENANT ANDRÉ TOGO

1. What is the best thing about being a Salvation Army officer?

This is subjective, right? I think being a Salvation Army officer is about life and ministry. It is neither the name "officer" nor the uniform that counts, but the officer's life and ministry. What counts is my life, André Togo, and not my uniform or my rank as a lieutenant. Every officer is judged according to his or her acts and works. And a good work can be despised because of bad behavior. As I understand it, an officer of The Salvation Army must have good behavior, worthy of a leader, of God's servant. Such behavior calls for certain spiritual, moral, intellectual, and social qualities.

2. What keeps you in officership when things are tough?

How marvelous it would be if all leaders placed Christ before all things! If we all served God and His people in a spirit of love, harmony, and humility! Unfortunately, that's not always the case. We are marked by sin, and our service is affected. At times we encounter tensions, problems, and frustrations in our officership. God's Word recommends that we accept, love, serve, and take care of one another. But on many occasions a tendency to deal with problems in a worldly manner takes over, often because of poor communication, especially in regard to making decisions and achieving goals. Difficulties are caused by our different personalities and temperaments, according to our background, habits, feelings, and experiences. Some think and act quickly, others think and act slowly. And when things are tough, we complain.

For me, learning to work with others in difficult situations is part of my sanctification process. It is not easy; it is often very laborious. But God gives the grace and wisdom to work with problematic leaders. When things are tough I'm always reminded of my calling in the Army as an officer. That's my source of consolation and strength, to know that I'm not in the ranks by myself, to know that I'm called to serve all kinds of people and leaders in joy and hardship, in favorable and unfavorable circumstances.

I made up my mind to endure and never give up, because the One whom I serve knows that I'm able. This word means a lot to me: "No temptation has overtaken you that is not common to man. God is faithful, and he will not let you be tempted beyond your ability, but with the temptation he will also provide the way of escape, that you may be able to endure it." (1 Corinthians 10:13 ESV)

As officers, we meet enormous difficulties in our ministry. The constant life of battle we lead forces us to stay in communion with God. We must be men and women of prayer in order to maintain a proper focus when things are tough.

3. What is the greatest move of God you have experienced in an appointment?

The Bible is filled with stories of people who lived their lives under the influence of God. Because of their deep faith and a willingness to serve, God used them to fulfill His purposes.

In my current appointment, at Amandas Corps in Concession, Zimbabwe, I have seen and am seeing the hand of the Lord upon my life and ministry in a very special way. I believe this move of God is due to my willingness to step out in faith and to face difficult situations for the glory of His Name. Upon our arrival, we found that many community members and some corps members were involved in syncretism and had intermarried with unbelievers. Through prayer and specific development initiatives aimed at community transformation, God powerfully led many to salvation and to great restoration.

4. What's the best innovation you've helped create or extend?

On the day of Pentecost, Peter, under the power of the Holy Spirit, reconfirmed the prophecy in the book of Joel concerning the pouring out of God's Spirit upon all flesh. He reiterated that young men will see visions and old men will dream dreams. The Wise Man of the book of Proverbs wrote, "Where there is no vision, the people perish." (28:19 KJV) George Barna writes in his book, Power of Vision: "Vision for ministry is a clear mental image of a preferable future imparted by God to His chosen servants and is based upon an accurate understanding of God, self and circumstances." He also related that Duke Ellington, the late jazz musician and bandleader, was once asked to provide a definition of rhythm. "If you got it," he replied, "you don't need any definition. And if you don't have it, there isn't a definition that will help."

To fulfill His purposes, God uses men and women through whom He implements His plan. By His choice, God expresses and exercises his sovereignty in the life of the one he uses as His instrument. He calls whom He wants, when and where He wants to, and in the manner He finds good. I cannot explain why I was the object of this choice for the implantation of The Salvation Army in Mali. I am not claiming to have been the creator of the Army in that country, But one thing remains certain: It was in a vision that the Lord spoke to me and called me to start The Salvation Army even though I had never before known or heard of a church or an organization of that name.

5. What's the best means of influence and how have you used it?

As officers, we influence—exercise an action on—the people we lead and those surrounding us in the community. Personally I influence without giving a command, without exercising pressure on people. I know they observe, they see and hear me doing what is necessary. Whenever I speak to them after leading by example, they give themselves; they work without pressure. They know who I am, they know what I am here for, and they know how deeply I love them, how dedicated I am to God's work, how polite, respectful, kind, discreet … And these things bring us closer to each other in confidence and with an open mind.

I believe there is no progress without unity. The Lord Jesus Christ prayed for all the believers to be one as He and the Father are one (John 17:20-23). This unity is not obtained by attending Salvation or Holiness meetings in the same room, wearing the same uniform, or singing in the same brigade. It is our hearts that should bind us together to see in the same direction, to desire the same thing, and reach out in love, hand in hand. Where there is love, there is unity; love is the glue of unity.

LIEUTENANT ANDRÉ MÉRÈ-BARA TOGO of the Zimbabwe Territory is from Mali, where he grew up in extreme poverty. At 13, he was accepted into seminary to become a Catholic priest, but when he was dismissed a year later without explanation, he turned from God to Satanism and fetishism. He met a fortune-teller who adopted him as a son and abused him for the next five years. Then, a blinding light appeared to him and God spoke directly to him about Jesus. In 2004, he became an ordained minister in New Life Ministries, Church of God in Christ. One day when he was praying, he got a vision of people in white uniforms playing trumpets surrounding his home country. When he awakened, he found The Salvation Army through a Google search. He was accepted to the War College in Vancouver, but wasn't able to get a visa, so he joined the Army's Regional Facilitation Team in Nigeria. In early 2007, he went with a team into Mali, where The Salvation Army had no presence, and he started the first class of 30 Army recruits. Togo was accepted as a cadet in the Democratic Republic of Congo Kinshasa in 2008 and was appointed to the Zimbabwe Territory with his wife, Fatouma. He currently serves as corps officer of the Amandas Corps.

GIVING BIRTH TO SOMETHING WORTHWHILE

LT. COLONEL PAM TRIGG

1. What is the best thing about being a Salvation Army officer?

Bringing people into the Kingdom of God and teaching them to grow to be like Jesus.

Example: One day when I had small children at home and I was cooking in the kitchen, a knock came on the door. I looked a sight with an apron on and flour everywhere but went to answer, and the lady at the door asked me where The Salvation Army held their services. Someone had given her our address. The corps had no hall of its own, as it had been burned down two months before we took up our appointment. We met in an old wooden Scout hall. I invited the woman into my untidy kitchen and gave her the information she wanted. We talked a little about belief and God's plan for people to come to Him.

The woman attended on Sunday, was welcomed by the people in the corps, and came to a couple of Bible studies. On the next Sunday, she made her decision to become a Christian. Her husband then became a Christian and her daughter started Sunday School.

That woman is still a Salvationist who readily gives her testimony about what the Lord is doing in her life. I see her from time to time and as I look at her, I remember the day we met and the thrill I got when she became a soldier in the Army.

2. What keeps you in officership when things are tough?

In the early days of my officership, my husband died. The loss was devastating. Albert was 44 and was regarded as a future leader in the Army. Could anything be so hard to take? The fact that I believed God called me to be an officer kept me going, but realizing that God knew all about my life before I set out on this path was a great discovery.

God knows my beginning and my end, and I trust my life to Him. I might be surprised at what happens, but God is never surprised. God is not a puppet master, nor does He make things happen to test me. I can be confident that there is nothing in this world that can take me away from His plan for my life.

"I'm absolutely convinced that nothing—nothing living or dead, angelic or demonic, today or tomorrow, high or low, thinkable or unthinkable—absolutely nothing can get between us and God's love because of the way that Jesus our Master has embraced us." (Romans 8:38-39 *The Message*)

3. What is the greatest move of God you have experienced in an appointment?

When I was living in Hong Kong and my husband was the finance secretary, I had little to do other than look after my children. I wanted to be useful. I knew I was an officer, but I had no role that had anything to do with mission and ministry—until one day the social secretary asked if I could play the timbrel. Of course I could. I had even been a timbrel leader in a former life.

I started teaching timbrel playing to teenage girls in a correctional facility run by the Army. Every Monday evening I would go to Kwai Chung, go through all the security checks, and enter the building. Girls would come from everywhere. They hugged me and chattered away. Most of these girls had been arrested in brothels or they were thieves or beginning a life of crime. Their English was poor, with a lot of swear words thrown in, and my Cantonese was non-existent. After the practice I would have supper with Envoy Chu, the manager of the facility—coffee and frozen sponge cake with frozen jam filling. No one had ever told her that the cake needed to thaw before it was eaten.

Envoy Chu was highly regarded. She had received the Order of the Founder from General Arnold Brown at the Army's centenary celebrations in London. The correctional facility was neat and clean and very well run—a joy to visit. And Envoy Chu loved the girls. She taught them to sew and paint and exposed them to all kinds of arts and culture. She showed them Christ in action. She demonstrated Christian servanthood. She prayed with the girls. As I attended week after week, I saw them change from aloof, suspicious, superstitious girls to bright, cheerful, lovely young women waiting to attack the next phase of their lives. Many became Christians and many went on to become good citizens, wives, and mothers.

I was able to be part of a life-changing program in a colony that had made money its god and that had no place for these girls. Slowly and quietly these young women learned about Jesus Christ and his love for them. It revolutionized their lives.

4. What's the best innovation you've helped to create or extend?

I never saw myself as a writer; I had no writing or publishing experience, and I had no desire to work in the editorial department. Yet I was appointed the national editor-in-chief. For the first year I complained almost every day about how I was not right for the appointment.

Officers complained about the publications ad nauseam, mostly because the black type came off on their hands and shirts when they sold them in the pubs. The contents were also criticized, and I felt persecuted. In the back of my mind I wanted to publish more modern papers. My dream was to make them more professional, with writing and photos that would attract people's attention and make them want to buy them.

I discussed this with the territorial commander, Commissioner Norman Howe, and with his encouragement and tons of planning, we eventually produced a new *Young Soldier* in color that we called *Kidzone*. A few months later the *War Cry* changed to magazine style, in full color. We also produced *OnFire* for Salvo readers.

I was delighted. I felt I had given birth to something worthwhile—a magazine that would start from something the reader could relate to and move to something the reader hadn't a clue about. *War Cry's* aim is to catch readers' attention, inform them, and present Jesus Christ to them.

Salvation Army officership has been a great lifestyle, and I have experienced the working of a great God in my life.

LT. COLONEL PAM TRIGG was born in Geelong, Victoria, in the Australia Southern Territory. She entered the training college from Geelong West Corps in 1971 with her husband, Albert. They served in corps before going to Hong Kong 1974, where Albert was appointed the command's finance secretary. They returned to Australia and commanded the Northcote Corps before being appointed to the staff of the training college. Albert was promoted to glory in 1983. Following that, Pam served in corps and divisional appointments as well as being the first full-time chaplain at the Army's Bethesda Hospital in Melbourne. She was the divisional commander of the Melbourne Central Division and the national editor-in-chief before she retired. Pam has three children and six grandchildren.

ABLE TO SERVE 24/7

LT. COLONEL BARBARA HUNTER

1. What is the best thing about being a Salvation Army officer?

The fact that I am able to serve 24/7. I do have to work at keeping a balance with my family life, but when I consider that I am free to serve and that God can call on me at any time of the day—that's great.

Examples: Being called at 5:30 a.m. to be with a family with a dying relative; being called at 11:30 p.m. to minister to a family whose relatives have been in a serious car accident ... I could go on and on.

2. What keeps you in officership when things are tough?

A strong sense that I am called to serve in the Army.

There have been times of great frustration and doubt, but I have always come back to the strong inner sense that I have to trust and move forward. At my age it is easier to look back and see how those times have proved valuable in my spiritual growth and deepened my commitment.

3. What is the greatest move of God you have experienced in an appointment?

I don't believe I have seen one "great move," but rather continually seen the moving of God in the lives of people who have really done a 180. I have seen miracles in the form of changed lives many times. One example is the total transformation of an addicted street-living woman who came to know Jesus. She "cleaned up" into a beautiful woman who reconnected with her family, is living a productive life, and is leading others to Christ. That is a MIRACLE. Who wouldn't want to be a part of a transformation from death to life?

4. What's the best innovation you've helped create or extend?

My husband, Bill, was the innovation piece of our officership. He often thought outside the box with a true desire to be sure the Army was relevant. Serving that way was not easy. I felt I played an important role in supporting and encouraging him. Many of the new initiatives he helped birth and tried to move forward have not survived. That is sad for me.

5. What's the best means of influence and how have you used it?

When I was a divisional commander, I worked hard at listening to my officers, and even though we had to work within the system and the structure, I was willing and open to new programs and how we would approach them.

Commissioned in 1968 in the USA Western Territory, **LT. COLONEL BARBARA HUNTER** earned a B.S. degree in organizational management and Christian leadership from Colorado Christian University, and served on the School for Officer Training faculty. She served in Russia while appointed to the USA Western Territory. She then served in the USA Eastern Territory as prayer ambassador, territorial personnel secretary, and divisional commander in Southern New England. She retired as an officer of the USA Eastern Territory and is now living in Tucson, Arizona, where she is active in Army work.

TOUGH TIMES, TERRIFIC TIMES

COMMISSIONER JOE NOLAND

1. What is the best thing about being a Salvation Army officer?

For me the best thing about being a Salvation Army officer can be summed up in one word: Opportunity! In the Western world especially, the Salvation Army brand opens doors that are less accessible to the clergy—or most others for that matter: evangelism, fundraising, public relations, influence, whatever. Here are three examples.

As a corps officer: During the racially explosive 1960s and early '70s, Doris and I—two white officers—planted a corps in a segregated black community. We visited every home in that community, in uniform, building a Sunday School congregation averaging 300 per week (parents included) and enrolling some 250 junior soldiers and 100 senior soldiers within two years. The doors of those homes were readily opened to us because The Salvation Army was trusted. It had little to do with us personally.

After one year, during a very hot summer with race riots exploding across the country, a Black Panther group came into the community thinking they could stir things up and turn everyone against these two "whiteys." To their chagrin, we had almost unanimous support in the community. I was the only white pastor to participate in a city-wide memorial service for Martin Luther King, Jr., after his assassination. It was because of the Salvation Army brand that we were afforded these unprecedented opportunities.

As a general secretary: The Billy Graham Association approached The Salvation Army asking if we would produce Billy's 50th Anniversary Celebration in Los Angeles. They wanted all proceeds to go to the Army for its work in the greater LA area. I was the officer responsible for producing the event at the Beverly Hilton Hotel. Again, this represented an unprecedented opportunity, producing an event honoring Billy Graham, one of my heroes.

As a territorial commander: I met with President George W. Bush three times—in the White House, in Philadelphia, and in Portland, Maine. In Portland, the President and his retinue toured the Salvation Army's community senior program. For 15 minutes, he stood with Janet and Rick Munn (the divisional leaders), Doris, and me talking about spiritual things while his Secret Service agents stood waiting across the room. We concluded that conversation by holding hands and praying together. Again, an opportunity we wouldn't have had except for being officers in The Salvation Army.

2. What keeps you in officership when things are tough?

The certain knowledge that God's timing is always perfect and that "tough" times are always a prelude to "terrific" times, so long as we hang in there and remain faithful. In the years leading up to training, I had read Norman Vincent Peale's *The Power of Positive Thinking* and put his teachings into practice. I learned early on that "Attitude is everything." Three things kept me going: (1) positive thinking; (2) faithful perseverance; and (3) a life partner who always maintained a healthy spiritual balance, thereby keeping me in balance through the tough times.

The most trying time of my officership career came during a DHQ staff appointment under a very controlling regime. This was the only time I ever entertained the thought of leaving. It was a two-year appointment, and six months into it, when I was at my lowest point ever, the chief secretary came to town and personally handed me my appointment as a delegate to ICO. God's timing couldn't have been more perfect, even if I had written the script. My self-esteem had never been lower nor my body weight higher. I returned spiritually refreshed, emotionally strong, and 30 pounds lighter.

During that time, God gave me a clear vision for the future—and it was to be within The Salvation Army. This was the only time we would ever ask for a change of appointment—to a corps, expecting to remain on the field until we retired. We were granted that request, which again proved to be the right appointment coming at exactly the right time. The rest is history. There would be other tough times later on, but God's perfect will and perfect timing carried us through. With that in mind, we would have happily stayed in corps work until the (R) was placed after our name. Attitude is everything. Besides, where else would we have had such extraordinary opportunities?

3. What is the greatest move of God you have experienced in an appointment?

I'm tempted to say the move of a DC, and that would be partly right, as with the new one coming we were released to allow God's moving to flow freely through our Spirit-granted giftedness, opening the way for some miraculous outpourings.

Our first appointment was to plant a new corps at a time when there had been no new corps plants for decades. This was 1965, and there were no church growth conferences to attend, books to read, or tapes to listen to. We had to fly by the seat of our (uniform) pants, so to speak. The DC had set it all up for us in the traditional way: A storefront in the wrong location downtown, no parking available, no homes nearby, etc. "Put up a sign, place an ad in the paper, and pray for the people to come," he said. We suggested some creative alternatives. He said "No!"

He farewelled six months later. The new DC said "Yes!" We broke the lease on the building and started meeting in a school auditorium, which was given to us free all weekend, beginning Friday evening with youth activities. On Sunday afternoons and a weeknight we were given a community center in a housing project for a second corps plant operating simultaneously. This was before the Church Growth movement, and using schools or public facilities for worship hadn't been thought of. Downtown office space was also donated. No overhead costs at all.

The Spirit moved miraculously and fast. One set of statistics was recorded, but they were really two separate corps. We averaged 150–200 in Sunday School weekly and enrolled more than 100 junior soldiers and 50 senior soldiers the first year.

After being sent to Santa Ana, California, a large traditional band and songster corps, we introduced Evangelism Explosion (EE); four local officers accompanied me to Fort Lauderdale for training. Again, God moved miraculously. We were leading people to Christ in their homes. Those people would become part of the EE program and begin leading others to Christ. Twice yearly we were enrolling more than 100 new recruits at a time, on a Sunday evening, with a birthday celebration following. We had a birthday cake, the band would play, and each new soldier would be welcomed individually and applauded as they entered the auditorium. This was groundbreaking, exciting stuff:

500 senior soldiers, 100 active adherents, an average of 300 in Sunday School and 400 in Holiness Meeting.

Out of this came a Hispanic corps, which grew so large it forced the Anglo congregation to relocate. That's now the Tustin Ranch Corps. The Spanish–language congregation took over the facility and became one of the largest Hispanic corps in the country. By the way, they recently instituted an English–language service on Sunday afternoons.

4. What's the best innovation you've helped create or extend?

This is hard because there were so many, but it probably would be the innovative approach to Sunday School that we created in order to reach children at risk. It took many forms and shapes, depending on the needs of each local population, and became SONday'SCOOL, introduced by the film, "Altars in the Street." I wrote about the innovative beginnings in my book, *No Limits Together*.

5. What's the best means of influence and how have you used it?

Example and empowerment are the best means of lasting, productive influence. You can mandate, thereby influencing a person to act in certain ways, but it will generally not be productive or lasting.

Those who said "No" influenced me negatively, those who said "Yes," positively. I attempted to exemplify this kind of empowering leadership. General Paul Rader's favorite influencing phrase, and mine as well, was, "Go for it!" One effect might be the many innovations in the USA Eastern Territory on our watch, including a record opening of new corps.

Hopefully, I influenced some others to adopt the same empowering attitude. I think so.

COMMISSIONER JOE NOLAND and his wife, Commissioner Doris Noland, from the USA Western Territory, are retired but still fully engaged in the "no strings attached" creative process. Joe began his lifelong ministry adventure as the "garbage scraper" at Mt. Crags Camp in Malibu, California, and concluded his official "active" part of that adventure as territorial commander of the USA Eastern Territory. Doris began as babysitter/bugler at Camp Trestle Glen, Oregon, and concluded her official sojourn as associate territorial leader. Joe's ministry can be summed up in three words: chaos, creativity, and controversy, three elements implicit in any successful innovative endeavor. Cecil B. DeMille, renowned producer of biblical epics, once wrote, "Creativity is a drug I cannot live without." Joe's mantra reads, "Creativity is my drug of choice."

A CONCENTRATED LIFESTYLE

MAJOR STEPHEN COURT

1. What is the best thing about being a Salvation Army officer?

You get to invest all of your time, energy, passion, gifts, skills, and abilities into the Salvation War. Of course, every Christian should be involved "full time" in the Salvation War, whether employed as a plumber or teacher or mechanic or ... So, as an officer, I am not distinct in that I am involved in "full-time" salvation warfare, but in that I am engaged in *vocational* salvation warfare and leadership.

I was captured by this in younger days when volunteering at a Christian camp. The schedule was such that for every waking minute (it seemed) I was either taking it in—"doing my rations" (personal devotions) before the kids in my cabin woke up, doing staff devotions before the kids in the cabin got going, listening to the preachers or participating in corporate worship—or giving it out—evangelizing, teaching Christianity, discipling. I thought that this was the ideal system: concentrated strategic Christianity. Camp counseling works during summers when you can afford to volunteer a couple of weeks. Officership provides this opportunity for life.

2. What keeps you in officership when things are tough?

Tough? It's always tough! It's usually tiring. And it often sets one up as an attack target. But here are a few things that help:

- You have to love it. I love it. I love the concentrated lifestyle. I love the fact that officership offers potentially more impact than any other life choice.
- Death to self. That's the negative side of holiness. But if you're dead to self, the influence of tough, tiring, targeted temptation is minimized.
- Two quick truths: (1) You are not your rank. (2) You are not your appointment. This helps put things in perspective.

3. What is the greatest move of God you have experienced in an appointment?

Once, I was blessed to be fighting at a corps where the corps council went away for a weekend to pray up the strategy and goals for the following year. One of the goals was to see 365 conversions during the year! Wow! As one of the corps officers, I arranged to secure 365 copies of the initial follow-up materials we were using at the time.

To cut a 365-day story to the end, we failed miserably. But 153 people got saved that year. (That's the number of fish that certain disciples caught on a special day.) Hallelujah!

In another corps we engaged in the Army's 24/7 prayer relay, having committed to one week. We had eight three-hour shifts each day and by the end, God was stirring us up so much we hoped He might let us continue beyond the week. It turned out that we went three and a half years in prayer nonstop in a very strategic location in the neighborhood to drive the salvation war on that front. Praise the Lord!

4. What's the best innovation you've helped create or extend?

Well, one is The War College in Vancouver, which has accelerated other innovations in extraordinary prayer, outpost multiplication, primitive Salvationism, incarnational warfare, discipleship, cell-based systems, and revolution—and which is expanding around the world.

5. What's the best means of influence and how have you used it?

I'm not a big Internet guy, but its popular advent in the '90s coincided with some early influence: the corps at which we were appointed won the only IHQ Salvation Army website of the year competition. That brought opportunity to extend influence through websites, blogging, Twitter, podcasts, Facebook, Salvocasts, and so on.

I've been intentional and consistent on content. God has blessed the efforts.

MAJOR STEPHEN COURT of the Canada & Bermuda Territory, aims to win the world for Jesus through prayer, evangelism, discipling, holiness, networking, and various media.

A SENSE OF 'OUGHTNESS'

GENERAL JOHN LARSSON

1. What is the best thing about being a Salvation Army officer?

Knowing that, with God's help, you are making a difference in the lives of people. The difference can be dramatic—I've sometimes stood in awe when God has turned someone's life around and I have had some minor part to play in that. Or the difference can be smaller—someone who thanks you after you have preached for speaking directly to their need. But you have made a difference. And that is the best part of being an officer.

2. What keeps you in officership when things are tough?

What has kept me in officership when the storm winds have blown is a strong sense of "oughtness" that tells me that this is where I ought to be, never mind any present difficulties or disappointments. Whether one calls it a conviction or a calling or a sense of "oughtness," it all adds up to the same thing: a strong sense that this is where I should be. Someone once said: "Don't get off the train in the tunnel." When the train has sometimes gone into the dark, it is that sense of "oughtness" that has stopped me from getting off—and I have never failed to be surprised at how quickly the train emerges again into the light of day.

3. What is the greatest move of God you have experienced in an appointment?

Freda, my wife, and I always look back on our four years as the corps officers of Bromley Temple Corps in South London, England, with special gratitude to God. I write about it in my autobiography, *Saying Yes to Life:*

> God blessed our ministry there in a singular way. Ours was the privilege of experiencing something akin to what happened in the Early Church, as described in the Book of Acts: 'Day by day the Lord added to their number those whom he was saving' (Acts 2:47, *New English Bible*). New people came—sometimes directly through our activities but as often as not quite spontaneously—and found the Lord. At one point we noticed to our surprise that we had been enrolling on average a new soldier from outside the corps every month.

4. What's the best innovation you've helped create or extend?

I suppose there can only be one answer: the increased use of musical drama in the Army to present the Gospel. When John Gowans and I began writing musicals together, we were both corps officers, and at first I wondered whether I was being diverted from the *real* ministry of corps officership. But a fellow corps officer convinced me that if God had given me a gift it was because he wanted me to use it—and I found, to my inner relief, that by rigorous discipline of time I could fulfill my ministry as a corps officer and add the writing and producing of musicals as an "extra." In fact, that set a pattern for my whole officership: music has always been an addition to my main appointments. But John and I often commented that when we arrive in Heaven and the Book of Life is opened, we are likely to discover that we have influenced more people by the "extra" in our lives than by what we have achieved in our main appointments.

5. What's the best means of influence and how have you used it?

Ministering to people at their time and point of need is the key to being used by God. Sometimes that can be very practical—for example, being with someone when they are passing through a time of deep distress, or being a sounding board for someone who faces a difficult decision in life. Sometimes it can be more indirect—being sensitive to the needs of a congregation and having the right word of encouragement or challenge. At other times it can be by the use of whatever creative gifts God has given us—and all of us without exception are gifted in some way or other. In my case it has been through writing or composition of music. I treasure each occasion when people have shared with me that some article or book I have authored or some song I have composed reached their hearts when they most needed it.

GENERAL JOHN LARSSON, from the United Kingdom with the Republic of Ireland Territory, was world leader of The Salvation Army from 2002 to 2006. Swedish by nationality, he served with his wife Freda in corps, youth and training work in Britain, as chief secretary in South America West, and as territorial commander in the UK, New Zealand, and Sweden, after which he became Chief of the Staff at International Headquarters. He graduated from London University with a B.D. degree and is the author of *Doctrine Without Tears, The Man Perfectly Filled with the Spirit, Spiritual Breakthrough, How Your Corps Can Grow, Saying Yes to Life* (his autobiography), and *1929—A crisis that shaped The Salvation Army's future.* He is a composer of music and, together with General John Gowans, co-authored 10 full-length musicals.

'LORD, THIS IS IT!'

COMMISSIONER KAY RADER

1. What is the best thing about being a Salvation Army officer?

Knowing that God's will for my life was officership and obeying that call, despite the challenges. As an officer, I have never been bored on the job or watched the clock. Salvation Army officers will die of something, but never boredom.

As a field training officer in the Korea Territory, I traveled every Wednesday with a brigade of cadets to Shillim dong, an area in Seoul designated by the government as a camp for war refugees. Meetings were held in a military–style tent.

When the officers arrived at their appointment, they had discovered there was no water in the area. One had to walk long distances over the mountain to fetch it. The captain told us that water "soundings" had yielded nothing. One day as we were discussing the problem, I spied a small trickle at the edge of the tent. With solicited donations we were able to get a well dug, and to everyone's amazement water gushed up, more than enough to meet their needs. A miracle! Using funds realized from charging people in the area a pittance for the water, they were able to open a corps day care center.

Another miracle occurred following the birth of the couple's baby girl. When she was only one day old, I knew that little Susie was seriously ill. We were able to get immediate help for her, and she survived. Recently I met Captain Susie, now married. She said, "God gave me back my life, so I wanted to give Him mine through service in the Army." The best thing about being a Salvation Army officer? Witnessing miracle after miracle and later witnessing firsthand the harvest of seeds planted so very long ago.

2. What keeps you in officership when things are tough?

Part DNA—I'm not a quitter. Part Dedication—for me, covenant spells "staying the course." Part Devotion—my love for the Army and its mission has grown stronger over the years.

There was a time in recent history when married women officers were often either neglected or forgotten altogether by administration. This happened to me, causing me great pain and a deep sense of loneliness and rejection. It came very close to driving me to the breaking point.

Instead, passing through this deep valley led me to a mountaintop experience through Paul's testimony in Galatians 2:20: "I have been crucified with Christ and I no longer live, but Christ lives in me. The life I now live in the body, I live by faith in the Son of God, who loved me and gave himself for me." A friend referred to this verse as 220 voltage. For me, it was that powerful. Following the shortest prayer of my life, "Lord, this is it!"—a total surrender—my heart, attitude, and perspective on life, including officership, were changed. Since that moment, whether with or without appointment, I have followed the counsel of Hebrews 12:1,2: "… let us throw off everything that hinders and the sin that so easily entangles. And let us run with perseverance the race marked out for us, fixing our eyes on Jesus, the pioneer and perfecter of faith."

When things are tough, my focus is His internal presence as opposed to the ever-troubling externals.

3. What is the greatest move of God you have experienced in an appointment?

It happened during my appointment as acting territorial president of women's organizations (TPWO) in the Korea Territory. Christians from all denominations banded together to convene an unprecedented four-day convocation of believers, '80 World Evangelization Crusade. Fifty seminars were held in various locations across the city during the day, and in the evening two million people gathered for a service of celebration, seated cross-legged on a paved runway maintained by the government for use in case of an attack from North Korea.

Dr. Kim Joon Gun, director of Asia Campus Crusade and co-coordinator of the event, invited me to be the teacher of a "School of Prayer" to be held exclusively for women in the auditorium of one of Seoul's largest and most prestigious girls' high schools. My assignment was to speak each morning to a capacity crowd of 3,000. For me as an American, this was a daunting challenge for various reasons, not the least of which was the fact that Korean Christian women are renowned prayer warriors. Beyond that, Dr. Kim insisted that I give the presentation not in my native tongue, English, but in the Korean language. Furthermore, some of the women denominational leaders were unconvinced as to Dr. Kim's choice.

God broke through the resistance from the very first morning, calming these leaders' nerves and pouring out His spirit upon the delegates. Despite torrential rains they filled the auditorium daily without fail. The evening as well as the morning hours were anointed by the Holy Spirit. The goal of evangelization was realized. When he heard that two million souls were gathering at Yo Oui Do island for meetings each evening, one man in an elevator in a Seoul hotel was overhead to say, "That's scary!" It was that powerful.

4. What's the best innovation you've helped create or extend?

The innovation I hold most dear and would like to have been able to extend further is creating or reopening egalitarian gender opportunities for women officers, particularly married women officers. The chapter title "The Married Officer and His Wife" in the O & R for Officers was revised to "The Married Officer" and appropriate revisions made. Married women officers were given rank in their own right, and the quota for lieutenant colonel and above ranks was increased to include the wife along with the husband, thereby ensuring married women commissioners membership on the High Council. In tandem with this decision, headquarters board and council systems were revised to include married women officers.

As world president of women's organizations (now ministries), my primary goal was to keep the dream of Catherine Booth alive. This was realized in a number of ways, for which I am grateful to God and to my husband, who was more than supportive. Some of the changes may have appeared to be only "cosmetic." But during an Easter morning gathering in the Bomas Center, Nairobi, Kenya, a Kenyan male officer relieved our minds of this notion when he said from the platform that he was grateful to me for giving their married women officers rank in their own right. In certain cultures the authenticity of the married woman depends upon the husband to the extent that she is rendered a nonperson when he dies. Giving a married woman rank in her own right alleviates some of the pain that the cultural system creates for her.

5. What's the best means of influence and how have you used it?

Influence is needed on more than one level, but care must be taken to influence properly. Compared with exerting influence over those who look up to you as their leader, influencing leaders with higher rank and with authority over you will need special handling.

Influencing both levels on gender issues has taken me in several directions. The Army offers unique opportunities to share ministry across gender lines, whether married or single, but this principle is not always honored in practice by higher levels of leadership. It is important that women demonstrate professional credibility as authentic members of the team. I have tried to model shared ministry by actively participating alongside my husband. Hopefully some have been influenced to make full proof of their calling by seeing the possibilities of full participation in ministry by married women.

The ministry of encouragement offers another avenue of influence. I keep in touch with a group of younger women officers; I write to them, speak a word of encouragement, and keep up with their progress in the fight. Modeling effective leadership is another means of influence.

When as TPWO I realized that all too many women officers in the USA Western Territory lacked self-confidence as professional clergywomen, I vigorously promoted the first-ever Wesleyan Holiness Women's Clergy Conference, sending more than 100 women officer delegates. Women officers have been encouraged to attend Christians for Biblical Equality conferences as well.

Influence comes in a variety of packages. On the issue of gender equality I have tried to be consistent in pointing out blatant inconsistencies and insensitivities when no one seemed to notice. In addition to "speaking out" on issues, I think it is important to take advantage of every possible means of communication, written or spoken, whether within or outside the Army.

COMMISSIONER KAY F. RADER, from the USA Eastern Territory, is the former world president of women's organizations for The Salvation Army. She, with her husband, Paul A. Rader, the 15th General of The Salvation Army, served as international leaders from 1994–99. She served 22 years in Korea and holds a B.A. from Asbury College as well as several honorary degrees: a D.D. from Asbury Theological Seminary (1995) and from Roberts Wesleyan College (1998), and a D.H.L. from Greenville College (1997).

The commissioner served as a member of the board of trustees for Roberts Wesleyan College in Rochester, N.Y., and for Asbury Theological Seminary from 1998–2002; on the board of directors, Christian Friends of Korea, 2001 to the present; and on the executive committee for the Religious Alliance Against Pornography. Following retirement in 1999, she became adjunct professor at the E. Stanley Jones School of World Missions and Evangelism, Asbury Seminary. She is a member of the Overseas Ministry Study Group in New Haven, Connecticut. She and her husband are on the board of reference for Christians for Biblical Equality. They were the recipients of CBE's Lifetime Achievement Award (2007) for their courage and vision in advancing the biblical basis for equality.

PART THREE

STILL NOT CONVINCED?

THY KINGDOM COME

Let's be clear: We believe in the priesthood of all believers. The only difference between officers and other soldiers is availability. As Salvationists, soldiers and officers alike, we have one main goal: establishing God's Kingdom on Earth.

Are you sold on the premise? Listen to Army Founder Catherine Booth.

> The decree has gone forth that the kingdoms of this world shall become the kingdoms of our Lord and of His Christ, and that He shall reign whose right it is, from the River to the ends of the earth. We shall win. It is only a question of time. I believe that this Movement shall inaugurate the great final conquest of the Lord Jesus Christ.

William and Catherine Booth intended that the Kingdom of God spread to encompass the whole world! That remains our mission today. And it's not just some whim of the Booths. The Kingdom of God is a main theme of the New Testament.

In fact, it's a magnificent obsession. Jesus Himself was obsessed with it.

- His first preaching was on the Kingdom of God (Mark 1:15).

- The first request in the Lord's Prayer is "Thy kingdom come" (Matthew 6:10).
- He taught that our first priority is to "seek first his kingdom and his righteousness … " (Matthew 6:33).
- The first evangelistic campaign on which He sent His 12 apostles focused on healing the sick, driving out demons, and preaching the Kingdom (Matthew 10:1,7).
- The first evangelistic campaign of the 72 disciples was focused on healing the sick and proclaiming the Kingdom of God (Luke 10:9).
- The Kingdom was the main agenda item on His itinerary. Jesus went through Galilee preaching the Good News of the Kingdom, healing every disease, and casting out demons. (Matthew 4:23, 24).
- The Kingdom was the main subject of His teaching. Two of His "Blesseds" in the Beatitudes belong to those who will receive the Kingdom of God (Matthew 5:3,10).
- At least seven of His parables were based on the Kingdom of God (Matthew 13).
- Jesus evaluated people by their status in the Kingdom of God (Matthew 5:19).
- After His resurrection He talked about—you guessed it—the Kingdom (Acts 1:3).

FOCUS ON MISSION

It wasn't just Jesus who was so enamored with the Kingdom of God. Philip, the first missionary, preached the Good News of the Kingdom of God in Samaria (Acts 8:12). Paul went to Ephesus and for three months argued persuasively about the Kingdom (Acts 19:8). Later he went to Rome and explained and proclaimed the Kingdom and taught about the Lord Jesus (Acts 28:23, 31).

Are we agreed? The Kingdom of God is a pretty important aspect of what Jesus was trying to do, and of what those who followed Him were accomplishing.

So it's important. But what is it?

A kingdom is a "territory ruled by a sovereign; royal authority; sphere of influence" (Webster's). Those of us who belong to Jesus are part of that territory, under that authority, within that sphere of influence.

The Holy Spirit acts as more than just a spiritual customs agent to admit us into the Kingdom. The Holy Spirit sets up our new identity, living arrangements, and vocational responsibilities. The Kingdom is not a matter of talk but of power (1 Corinthians 4:20). It's not about talking for the sake of hearing ourselves speak. It's about backing up proclamation of the Gospel with demonstration of the Gospel! Yet it's not something that can be observed with the physical eye, because it is within us (Luke 17:21). It is personal, because God calls us into it (1 Thessalonians 2:12). Yet John describes himself as our companion in the suffering and the Kingdom, so it obviously has a corporate element to it (Revelation 1:9).

How can we recognize the Kingdom?

There are signs. Jesus instructed, "If I drive out demons by the power of the Spirit of God, then the kingdom of God has come upon you" (Matthew 12:28). The example and mission of Jesus and His disciples demonstrate that when the Kingdom is preached, signs and wonders such as healing and deliverance happen. Not only is there authority for it, there is an expectation of it.

Other signs include righteousness, peace, and joy in the Holy Spirit (Romans 14:17). These and other fruits of the Spirit characterize citizens of the Kingdom. Those who serve Christ in this way are "pleasing to God" (Romans 14:18). God loves this stuff.

Maybe you're confused about now. Maybe you're saying, "But I don't have that! I'm a Christian, but I'm not that joyful, I haven't suffered, and I've sure never healed anyone or kicked out any demons."

Here's the good news: This is not a test; it's not a standard you are measured against. Don't worry. Ask God for help. He delights in giving you His Kingdom (Luke 12:32)! Hallelujah! He will love it when He begins to see characteristics of His Kingdom in your life. Here's to living out the Kingdom in your neighborhood and spreading it until Catherine Booth's prophecy is fulfilled!

And while we acknowledge and celebrate specific callings to the role of plumber or accountant or teacher or ... we are convinced that many of us can optimize the days God has lent to us through officership as vocational extremism. Are you ready to join the band of mighty warriors?

WANTED, BUT NOT NEEDED?

Now, just in case you are getting the feeling, based on everything we have said so far, that we are getting desperate in recruiting you for officership, this "want ad" from George Scott Railton should put things in perspective.

WANTED ALWAYS

TO BECOME

OFFICERS IN THE SALVATION ARMY,

MEN AND WOMEN OF GOD

Anxious to devote their lives to the work of saving souls,

Whose characters will bear any amount of investigation;

Who can talk to a crowd of people out of doors and in, so as to wound sinners' hearts;

Who can lead a band of godly men and women to do anything likely to win souls;

Who are perfectly ready to speak, pray, visit, sit still, travel a hundred miles, or die at any moment;

Who have given up drink, tobacco and finery, for Christ's sake, or are willing to give up anything and everything for Him;

Who are willing to be led and taught, and to be sent home again if they do not succeed;

Who are willing to be evil spoken of, hated and despised, and even to be misrepresented, misunderstood, and undervalued at headquarters.

THE FOLLOWING NEED NOT APPLY:

Persons who, "being out of employment, desire to give themselves entirely," etc.;

Who "do not think they can be expected" to exhaust all their strength in laboring day and night to save souls;

Who, "if engaged, will endeavor to give satisfaction to their employers";

Who will take any notice of the fact that their "friends object" to their going or living anywhere or doing anything they are asked to do;

Who desire "light employment," "find their work begin to tell on them," etc.;

Who would like to know "particulars as to salary, hours, home, etc., before engaging";

Who "are sometimes troubled with doubts" about the inspiration of the Bible, the divinity of Christ, the Atone-
ment, election, the possibility of falling from grace,
eternal damnation, or the personality of the devil.

Who "having had considerable experience" in our kind of
work, think they know how to do it.

—*Heathen England*, 1879

Too often The Salvation Army has erred in begging "cap in hand"
for people to sign up as officers. The saying goes, "If you have to beg
them to come, you'll have to beg them to stay." And that does not an
extreme army of mighty warriors make.

So, let's clarify here and now. We "want" you, as George Scott Railton's officership pitch makes startlingly clear. But we don't "need"
you. The Salvation Army does not "need" you. It will advance quite
well without your red epaulets.

That said, you "need" The Salvation Army. If you are an officer
right now, you need the Army—and we're not talking about room and
board. If you are a soldier right now, without a specific calling to do
something else vocationally and strategically in the Salvation War,
you also "need" The Salvation Army. Officer or soldier, you need the
Army as a means of exercising the gifts and abilities God has given
you, as a means of fulfilling the mission calling God has given you,
and as a means of optimizing the impact you can make in this world.

THE DEFAULT CALL

Well, we have presented a vision of Salvation Army officership
rather different from that prevalent in some circles in the Western
world. We recognize that to some extent we are speaking idealistical-
ly. But we have been captured by a standard that we believe God en-

ables individuals to attain. And we are left dissatisfied with anything less. In this next little bit, we're shooting at pre-officers, but we invite every officer to read it as well (again, maybe a timely refresher).

Back in our school days, other than wanting to be professional football players, my buddy and I (Steve) figured we had our future planned out. We would both become senators and receive honorary doctorates. That was our ambition. You see, in that era, Canadian senators had to show up to work at least three days a year and get paid until they died—and we could add letters behind our names without a sweat! My goals have changed. I now have two: (a) win the world for Jesus; and (b) love Jesus more than anyone else does.

What's your plan? What's your ambition? What are you doing with your life? To be honest, the senator/honorary doctorate route is probably not the way to go.

Maybe you have no ambition. Maybe you're just looking forward to meeting that someone. Settling down, finding a job. Maybe you have fallen into a rut in which you feel existentially stuck. Maybe not ...

You're a Christian. Jesus has forgiven your sins, and you have a vital relationship with Him. But what should you do with the rest of your life?

Perhaps you are waiting for "The Call" to officership. It's some kind of mystical thing, like maybe getting slammed in the brain with a message from God. For some, it seems to work that way. Praise God!

It didn't happen like that for Lt. Colonel Timothy Mabaso of South Africa.

> God did not speak to me as he spoke to Abraham, Moses, David, or Jeremiah, all of whom were great men of the Bible. Yet He spoke and called me from where I was, challenging me by the needs of the people I lived with every day—many of whom were my peers.

Perhaps for you too the need is the call. Screaming heaps of people are tumbling down into damnation. Your understanding of that reality is God's call to you. Don't throw away your life while you wait for the brain slam.

Of course, in any discussion of the call, you've got to mention the Founder. You know what he said? That you have to be called into something else if you're not going to be an officer! So basically, all able soldiers are automatically on the track toward officership, and God calls some of them to be teachers and plumbers and factory workers, but all the rest are to be officers. It's what we call the default call. If God's not calling you specifically to do something else, be an officer. Period.

More from General Booth:

> But who is to go? YOU. You who read this. Who else is there to go? ... You are saved. You say your sins are forgiven, and that you belong to the family of God. ... You say the promises apply to you; why not the commands? Have one, and shirk the other? Never, never, never! They are united. ... Do you say you are a child and not a servant? Don't talk nonsense. How can you be a child without a child's spirit? And is it not the very essence of the child's spirit to serve his Father, and seek his Father's interests, and carry out his Father's most sacred purposes? ... You must go yourself.
>
> —William Booth, *The General's Letters,* 1885

And again:

> 'Not called!' did you say? 'Not heard the call,' I think you should say. Put your ear down to the Bible, and hear Him bid you go and pull sinners out of the fire of sin. Put your ear down to the burdened, agonized heart of humanity, and listen to its pitiful wail

for help. Go stand by the gates of hell, and hear the damned en-
treat you to go to their father's house and bid their brothers and
sisters and servants and masters not to come there. Then look
Christ in the face—whose mercy you have professed to obey—
and tell Him whether you will join heart and soul and body and
circumstances in the march to publish His mercy to the world.

—William Booth, *The General's Letters*, 1885

What are you waiting for? Why are you holding back? We're here
to tell you that there is no life like officership. There's nothing we'd
rather be doing. As Jim says, "I know this is where God wants me.
Why would I let anyone or any situation distract me from my calling
in Christ Jesus?" Look, you get to duke it out with the enemy all the
time! You get to hide in the Word and then deliver it to the people.
Make a "Ten Most Wanted" list. Drag sinners from the edge of hell.
Pour yourself into them so they get trained up to become "dangerous"
soldiers of Jesus Christ. Be prepared for vocational extremism. When
Major ST Dula of India arrived in a corps where many had left, what
did he do? He set about leading the war.

> Though my health was very weak, I fasted many days and
> nights. I spent most of my time at the Mercy Seat in tears
> praying over the roll book of the corps. I carried the Army flag
> in the street, visiting the houses of Salvationists and non–Sal-
> vationists and kneeling down in their sitting rooms with the
> flag. After many months, a great revival broke out in the corps.

Is officership something you absolutely have to do? Hear Major
Kjell Karlsten:

> I couldn't be happy with just filling my life with anything less
> than those things that really matter, the truly important things.

> I find it difficult to produce much interest in things that are nothing more than entertainment for the present moment. For sure, I can watch a good movie—but as I'm doing it, I'm often restless, because it is not for real. It is not the real business. It is not really important.

Want to be involved 24/7 in the "real business"? We invite you to join us in the war as an officer in The Salvation Army. Is God specifically calling you to do what you are doing now? No? If you think you can hack it, apply today.

BE THE REVOLUTION

Catherine Booth's famous axiom applies here: "There is no improving the future without disturbing the present." This book may have disturbed you. We haven't intended to offend anyone by it, but we have intended to offend satisfied sensibilities and compromised character and measured mediocrity. We have intended to tip over the whole mistaken concept of officership as a comfortable lifestyle, as an easy career, and replace it with God's idea of officership as vocational extremism. And once you've committed to leading the war, there's no turning back. Says General Paul Rader, "We have often thought, *God called us in and it will take God to call us out of this spiritual vocation.*"

So, if you are an officer reading this, hold up the mirror. The exercise of writing it has forced us to do that. It can be an uncomfortable exercise. But, look, we live 80 or 90 years and then hit eternity. We run through this whole thing once. We don't get any do-overs. Why settle? Why settle for the status quo in your officership instead of turning the world upside down? Why look forward to 65 years of coasting through 40 hours a week when, even with eight hours of sleep a night, each week offers more than 100 hours for fighting the war? Why get wrapped up in the latest television show or sports season more than in the latest evangelistic opportunity or discipling group? Why subsist on maintenance when you can lead an army to take a town? Why aim for merely incremental growth instead of revolution?

Let's make Railton and Booth–Tucker our standard for incarnational sacrifice, Cadman and Booth our measure of strategic innovation, Brengle our basis for doctrine, and Joe the Turk our ideal for reckless daring. Let's embody officership as vocational extremism.

If you are considering officership, we encourage you to pray. Seek God's face. Don't be distracted by images of mediocrity that we officers may have modeled. Do what a retired officer advised Major Bezzant to do: "… nail the call of God upon [your] life for officership." See what is possible! See what God can do in and through the lives of utterly devoted mighty warriors! Let's be the revolution we want to see.

Officer's Covenant

MY COVENANT

CALLED BY GOD
to proclaim the Gospel of our Lord and Saviour Jesus Christ
as an officer of The Salvation Army

I BIND MYSELF TO HIM IN THIS SOLEMN COVENANT

to love, trust and serve him supremely all my days,

to live to win souls and make their salvation
the first purpose of my life,

to care for the poor, feed the hungry, clothe the naked,
love the unlovable, and befriend those who have no friends,

to maintain the doctrines and principles of The Salvation Army,
and, by God's grace to prove myself a worthy officer.

Done in the strength of my Lord and Savior, and in
the presence of [the following wording to be adapted
to local circumstances] the Territorial Commmander,
training college officers and fellow cadets.

MORE FROM THE AUTHORS

James and Stephen also wrote

One Day: A Dream for the Salvation Army (Los Angeles: Frontier Press, 2010).

One Thing: Win the World for Jesus (Melbourne: SALVO Publishing, 2008).

One Army (Los Angeles: Frontier Press, 2011).

Trilogy available as *One for All* (Los Angeles: Frontier Press, 2011).

James Knaggs

Blogs at: http://tcspeak.com/blog/

Tweets at: https://twitter.com/jimknaggs

Leads an online network: http://savn.tv

Stephen Court

Blogs at: http://www.armybarmy.com/blog.html

Tweets at: https://twitter.com/stephencourt

Corps website: sacrossroads.com

Other books by Stephen:

Boundless: Living Life in Overflow, with Danielle Strickland (Monarch Books, 2013). Available at amazon.com as paperback and Kindle book.

High Counsel: Jesus and John on leadership, with Joe Noland (Los Angeles: Frontier Press, 2012). Available at amazon.com.

A Field for Exploits: Training leaders for The Salvation Army, with Eva Burrows and David Dalziel, ed., (London: Salvation Books, 2012). Available at amazon.com as paperback and Kindle book.

Army on Its Knees: Dynamics of great commissioner prayer, with Janet Munn (London: Salvationist Publishing and Supplies Limited, 2012). Available at amazon.com as paperback and Kindle edition.

Greater Things: 41 days of miracles, with James Thompson (XP Media, 2011). Available at elijahshopper.com and amazon.com.

Boston Common: Salvationist perspectives on holiness, ed., (Blackburn, Victoria, Australia: Salvo Publishing, 2010).

Hallmarks of The Salvation Army, with Henry Gariepy (Alexandria, Va.: Crest Publishing, 2010).

Holiness Incorporated: beyond corporate integrity, with Geoff Webb and Rowan Castle (Blackburn, Victoria, Australia: Salvo Publishing, 2009).

The Uprising: A holy revolution? with Olivia Munn (Blackburn, Victoria, Australia: Salvo Publishing, 2007). Available at amazon.com.

Revolution, with Aaron White (Credo Press, 2005). Available as used book on amazon.com.

Proverbial Leadership: Ancient wisdom for tomorrow's endeavours, with Wesley Harris (Credo Press, 2004). Available as used book on amazon.com.

Be a Hero: The battle for mercy and social justice, with Wesley Campbell (Destiny Image, 2004). Available as Kindle book at amazon.ca.

Salvationism 101, with Danielle Strickland (Credo Press, 1999).